INTRODUCTION
TO PASTORAL CARE

Books by William V. Arnold
Published by The Westminster Press
  Introduction to Pastoral Care
  When Your Parents Divorce (Christian Care Books)
  The Power of Your Perceptions (Potentials: Guides
  for Productive Living)
In collaboration with Dixie McKie Baird, Joan Trigg
  Langan, and Elizabeth Blakemore Vaughan
  Divorce: Prevention or Survival

INTRODUCTION TO PASTORAL CARE

William V. Arnold

The Westminster Press
Philadelphia

BOOK DESIGN BY ALICE DERR

Published by The Westminster Press®
Philadelphia, Pennsylvania

PRINTED IN THE UNITED STATES OF AMERICA
9 8 7 6 5 4 3

Library of Congress Cataloging in Publication Data

Arnold, William V., 1941–
    Introduction to pastoral care.

    Bibliography: p.
    Includes index.
    1. Pastoral psychology. 2. Pastoral theology.
I. Title.
BV4012.A76   253.5   81–16092
ISBN 0–664–24400–9   AACR2

TO MY FATHER

Contents

Preface

In writing an introductory book in pastoral care, I am seeking to address several concerns. First, good pastoral care must be grounded in good theology. Theology without concrete expression is dead. Pastoral care carried out as mere technique without substantive "reasons" is shallow and subject to aimless wandering among new fads and approaches. Therefore, this book will call the reader to evaluate expressions of pastoral care in terms of his or her theological commitments. My own commitment to Reformed theology will no doubt show itself, but such a commitment on the part of the reader is not a requirement for the book to have usefulness.

Second, then, the book is intended to be *useful.* I am quite conscious of the number of times pastors, including me, have found writing in pastoral care to be focused on concerns of the specialists. Too little knowledge is shown of the more frequent locus of pastoral care—the community, where there is far less opportunity for structure or control. In that sense, the book is intended not only for the seminary student but for the pastor who is looking for connections between faith affirmations and the exercise of pastoral care. Illustrative material will be drawn from parish and community experiences more than the counselor's office.

Third, the traditions of pastoral care will be taken seriously. In my own teaching, the two books on which I have relied most frequently as texts in the field have been *The Christian Pastor,* by Wayne E. Oates, and *Basic Types of Pastoral Counseling,* by Howard J. Clinebell, Jr. Oates provides the reader/student with a masterful integration of pastoral identity and pastoral activity. Using the roots of developmental psychology and devoting serious attention to his theological and biblical heritage, he orients the pastor to the tasks with a firm footing. Clinebell provides us with a survey of approaches and thus gives the pastor alternatives from which to choose in carrying out the ministerial task with expertise and a sense of professionalism. This book is not a new or radical departure, nor is it a mere duplication of their efforts. It is an attempt to provide concrete expression to careful integration of theological and behavioral knowledge about human beings. That expression is, of course, pastoral care, which I have defined as the attempt to bring theology, or the "good news," to bear in a relationship where one is known as a member of the priesthood of all believers and seeks to care in a manner that is sensitive to the other person or persons and faithful to the theological commitments that have brought them together.

My thanks go to many people and institutions for making this writing time possible. Union Theological Seminary in Virginia has provided me with a sabbatical leave, and the Association of Theological Schools in the United States and Canada provided me with a grant to make fuller use of that leave. Wayne E. Oates arranged for me to have full academic resources and consultation at the University of Louisville School of Medicine and gave of himself in reading a major portion of the manuscript with faithfulness and candor. Milton and Callie Smith provided our family with living accommodations that afforded privacy and friendly support. Second Presbyterian Church of Louisville, Kentucky, where I once served as a pastor, welcomed us back and kept me in touch with the realities and possibilities of parish ministry. D. Cameron Murchison, my colleague and friend, provided theological critique of my work. Betty Hopkins and Sally Hicks helped see to it that all the mechanical aspects of getting a book ready for the publisher were accomplished. Most important, my wife and daughter saw to it that I never deserted the field of "real living" for the unreality of pure theory for too long.

W.V.A.

PART I
THE GROUND
OF PASTORAL CARE

1
Who Are We?
A Look at Human Nature

"Do something!" is all too often the watchword of the busy pastor. After all, with phone calls and visits bringing news of deaths, births, illnesses, cures, divorces, and reconciliations, who has time to sit down and think about it! The minister's job is to respond to all these experiences in the life of the congregation and the community. Right?

That is right. And something else is also true. The pastor is *called* to respond in a way that reflects accurately the nature of God and of us who are created in his image. There comes the rub! So this book begins with an attempt to clarify some of the crucial points in understanding that nature rather than with new ways to organize our time or new techniques to be used in each of these situations. Suggestions along these lines will come. First, however, it is important to establish some ground, or at least to take time to understand the ground on which we are already standing.

Pastoral care, if carried out well, responds to other persons in a way that takes them seriously at two levels, at least. The first is the level of who they believe themselves to be and the value which that belief attaches to them. The second level, and the focus of this chapter, is that we care for persons in terms of who we believe them to be according to our theological understanding and the regard in which they are held according to that belief.

Our theological assumptions about human nature affect the manner in which we relate to and care for other people in multiple ways, many of them beyond our awareness or understanding. A major thesis of this book is that we need to inspect those assumptions which we hold. Such reflection, in community as well as individually, will help us to evaluate our approaches to see if they are consistent with our assumptions. Further, reflection on our assumptions will serve as an opportunity for us to correct ourselves and continue to grow in the image in which we believe ourselves to be created. And we will be able to claim the regard in which we believe ourselves to be held.

THE GOODNESS OF HUMAN BEINGS

There are several useful frames of reference within which we can inspect our assumptions about human nature. The first focuses on our goodness—what we think is possible for human beings. "Human potential" has been a popular secular phrase for talking about this aspect during the last decade or so. The word "goodness" here carries a sense of what we are *capable* of doing and becoming more than a sense of what we are "worth" from a perspective of "value." Finitude and sin are crucial concepts for our discussion. What we believe about them has immense effect on the ways in which we encourage and discourage, support or ignore, push or give up in dealing with those for whom we care. In other words, what hope, if any, do we have to offer?

On one extreme, our beliefs about the goodness of human nature might identify problems as unsolvable hardships, confirming our helplessness and inability to achieve anything. On the other extreme, we might be too reassuring, leading people to believe that they can solve any difficulty. The two examples reflect extreme views of human depravity and unobstructed human potential. What are your beliefs about the goodness of human nature? How do you see them affecting the way in which you care for other people, or yourself? Is there a connection between what you claim to believe and your practice of caring?

Goodness and Limitations

It is my belief that we human beings are, by nature, limited creatures in need of God's grace. Those limitations are broad-based, extending to perception, ability to respond, ability to understand ourselves and others. While we all share these limitations and more, there are variations, such as different visual capacities, differing intellectual abilities, varied personal joys and tragedies which leave lasting effects. But we all share a common experience of having limits and their defining (limiting) characteristics.

Such a general view of limitations has several implications. It means that we are incapable of knowing exactly what another person needs, just as we are incapable of always knowing exactly what we need for ourselves. Such an awareness of limitations raises serious questions about attempting to "take over" another person's decision-making. It raises questions about how adequate we are to give advice in a demanding or authoritarian way. *Seeking to understand* becomes the first priority when we acknowledge limitations. As Wolfhart Pannenberg speaks of it, understanding requires the ability to think oneself into the position of the other person. We often call it empathy.

Seeking to understand is a natural outgrowth of the belief that we are limited creatures. When we experience limits, or "don't know," we try to find out, so our limitations actually create a bond between us as human beings. There are two kinds of bonds in particular. The first is a bond of *commonality.* We are all alike in that we are limited. That is a characteristic we hold in common. While a great deal of time and literature has been devoted to identifying us as unique, there is important reason to be reminded that we are also alike. Without that sense of "alikeness" there would be little reason for seeking to understand or to be understood. There would be no common ground. I, for instance, am far more inclined to become involved with someone who wants to learn, even if we differ, than with someone who presumes to "know all" and to have no interest in learning. So our limitations, when admitted, are a given bond of commonality which forms a link between us.

The second bond is that of *necessity*. We need each other. As limited creatures we are incapable of taking care of ourselves. Our limitations force us, whether we like it or not, to depend on each other.

Illustrations of these characteristics of commonality and necessity come frequently in pastoral care. After one Sunday morning in which the minister left out the creed in the worship service and, with a mixture of embarrassment and humor, had to return to it, a member of the church was heard to say, "That's the reason I can go and talk to him about mistakes I have made—he makes them too." Or, take the husband and successful businessman who sits in an office with the pastor and begins, "This is very difficult for me to say, because I have never let *anyone* know that I needed help for anything."

Goodness and Sin

Closing a discussion about the nature of goodness in human beings with the agreement that we are limited is not enough. It leaves room for some to say that all those limitations can be overcome. So, we must move quickly to a second important doctrine that concerns "goodness" in us —sin.

Definitions of sin are varied and complex, including ontological states, rules of propriety, definitions of will, views about impaired judgment, and the deliberate breaking of covenants. All of those perspectives can, with reasonable accuracy, be summarized under the rubric of distortion. To be a sinner is to be one who distorts a proper understanding of self, others, God, and the relationships that exist between them. Without the reality of sin, our limitations could be celebrated as a mechanism that brings us together in community. We could admit our finitude readily and move gratefully into sharing burdens and taking responsibility for our shortcomings.

With the ingredient of sin in our nature, however, such joyous communion does not always take place. The distortion affects both our willingness and our ability to acknowledge the places in which we fall short. It is the dynamic reality of sin that moves many of us to claim uniqueness and to ignore commonality. It is the isolating force of sin that leads us to believe that we do not need each other. That process leads us instead to be evasive and self-deceitful. One expression of deceit has appeared in the language of pride. Distorted pride claims uniqueness and the belief that we can take care of ourselves, and others, without need for external help.

Another expression of sin often can be seen in feigned helplessness and excessive dependence. Some writers have pointed out helpfully that much of the writing about sin as pride has been done by male theologians writing about other males, whether they recognized it or not. The sin unacknowledged by them was the helplessness and dependence too often seen in women. With the raising of consciousness over recent years, it is no longer accurate or appropriate to stereotype in such a way, but it is important to point out that both pride and dependence may deny and inhibit the bonds of commonality and necessity.

The reality of human finitude, in company with the reality of sin, affects the way in which we carry out pastoral care.

If not examined, our own limitations and sinfulness are catered to rather than kept in perspective as we go about our days of ministry. To maintain that a particular person "doesn't need" our help reveals a distorted view of finitude and sin. To operate as if everyone needs our help all the time reveals another!

Early in my training for ministry, working in a psychiatric hospital, I became aware of a physician whose personal characteristics resulted in his being avoided by patients and staff alike. Patients would skip appointments, staff would come late to meetings and leave early, and so did I! My supervisor pointed out that I should make him aware of what was happening. I resisted, fearful at the thought of such an encounter. Finally, after much prodding, I did so, and was amazed at the grateful response I received. He had seen the behavior on the part of patients and staff but had not known what the problem was. We worked together on friendly terms from that point on.

On reflection now, I can see that there were assumptions at work in me that went far beyond fear. One assumption was that a physician had no need of me and would, in fact, have no respect for what I might say. That was an assumption about commonality—I didn't believe that we had any. And it was an assumption about necessity—I didn't believe that he needed me. My limitations were overemphasized in my thinking. His were denied. My sin was evident in the distortion that tried to keep me out of an uncomfortable situation. Certainly, the end could have been different, but my beliefs and assumptions are examined much more frequently now than was the case before. Encounters that do not turn out so well call for that reflection, too.

Goodness and Gifts

The example above illustrates another facet of our nature as human beings. We, by acknowledging the characteristics of finitude and sin, also demonstrate abilities to perceive, to reflect, to decide, and to take action. We are people with gifts. Depravity does not contradict or exclude the presence of abilities. In acknowledging distortion within ourselves, we also demonstrate that we can, at times, see it. Just because we are limited in our capacity to perceive does not mean that we cannot perceive at all. Just because we distort our understanding does not mean that we are not capable of learning. Just because our actions are carried out poorly or for bad reasons does not mean that we are incapable of correcting or of being corrected.

We are called to confess our shortcomings as an affirmation of our capability of transcending ourselves, reflecting on and learning from our experience. We can apply the perceptions we gain through revelation. And so we also profess our ability, our capacity, and our possibilities. Our limits and our gifts serve as checks on each other.

Tendencies to emphasize one aspect over and against the other are always present. To overemphasize finitude relieves us of responsibility and acknowledgment of ability. To overemphasize sin teaches us, too, to escape responsibility in the guise of "not doing harm." On the other hand, overemphasis of the gifts ignores the limitations and poses real dangers as well. It seems most proper to identify all these realities in any discussion of human nature. We are both bound and free, limited and capable, prone to selfishness and selflessness, likely to love ourselves and our neighbor, bound both to disguise ourselves and to seek to become transparent. Those tensions are a theological reality that we claim. In the same breath we can say that we are fine and be fearful, say that we are angry and at the same time care.

Reflections on Goodness

It is important that we be cognizant of these multiple and complex characteristics in human nature when we are deciding whether to take initiative in a pastoral encounter. Without our doing so, there is likely to be more inconsistency and confusion for us and the other person than would otherwise be the case.

Take a few moments now to think about recent encounters you have had with persons in need or occasions in which you needed help. What were the assumptions about human nature and its goodness that influenced the action you took and what you expected? Were the actions and the assumptions congruent? Those assumptions affect us daily, and one aim of this book is to foster a regular process of reflection on them. This frame of reference about the goodness of human beings is only the first in our consideration of human nature.

THE DEVELOPMENTAL NATURE
OF HUMAN BEINGS

Just as we are affected in pastoral care by our assumptions about the *goodness* of humans, so we are affected by what we believe to be possible or likely in the *development* of human beings. How, theologically, do we believe that people grow? What do we believe motivates them to respond and change?

Developmentalism, often viewed as a psychological concept, is also theological. References are found throughout Scripture to the concept of maturing. Our modern-day understanding of the grief process, which is a developmental concept, is reflected in many of the psalms of lament, such as Psalm 22, 88, or 102. They describe stages through which people move in adjusting to loss.

Development and Change

We do have assumptions, often unexamined, about the way in which we should work with people educationally, pastorally, and in preaching. If our assumptions view growth as occurring in scattered spurts, prompted by dramatic external events, then we will care for people in a way that attempts to induce such dramatic experiences. Our theology, in such a case, places emphasis on helping people become aware of moments in which there is opportunity to respond. They will be encouraged to recognize those scattered occasions in which God is speaking to them or providing an experience designed for their growth in faith. A pastor so oriented will be present in a sensitive and powerful way with people when they are going through major crises in their lives. After all, these are opportunities for people to make important decisions and to become aware of new strengths and insights. A pastor who believes in the decisiveness of such moments will develop a good network for information so that she or he will be there when those times occur. Those are crucial "developmental moments."

All too often we adopt one doctrine or its implications to the exclusion of others that are equally important. The dimension discussed above, for instance, builds on a belief that conversion is the primary model to take into account when planning strategy for effective pastoral care. Rightly, it recognizes that crisis points are vulnerable points for men and women. They will make decisions at those points that carry important implications for their future. Any pastor who believes in the importance of giving special attention to people at tragic moments also believes in the importance and possibility of conversion as a real phenomenon in human living.

Development and Assurance

There are others in pastoral care who maintain that their task is not to bring about change but to bring assurance. Such individuals speak of the importance of bringing the good news that God loves the person, regardless of the response to tragedy. Ministers who are devoted to this approach pride themselves on not "expecting" anything of the person to whom they go. To do so would be to pressure them in an unfair way and, theologically, would be defining the person as the responsible agent in a spiritual pilgrimage, rather than God. So the pastoral task is to bring assurance rather than pressure. *Being* is more important than *doing.* A high view of God's act of justification through Christ has led many to view the function of *presence* as the prime factor in the exercise of pastoral care.

A great deal of helpful writing can be found about the power of presence without expectation in the pastoral encounter. Many nontheological writers, such as Carl Rogers, have developed techniques of caring that are quite helpful in this sphere.

Development and Formation

Another frame of reference for caring is drawn from the doctrine of sanctification. Human possibility and the importance of persons taking more responsibility for their own growth and development are highlighted here. The powers of conversion or justification are not ignored; rather, the person is called to play a more active role.

Another way of talking about this dimension is under the rubric of "character formation." Stanley Heurwas, in his book *Character and the Christian Life,* notes our tendency to shape the conceptions of the moral life around the metaphor of command. Thus, the obligation of the Christian is to be obedient to the will of God, always ready to obey each new command. However, "the language of command," he notes, "tends to be inherently occasionalistic with a correlative understanding of the self that is passive and atomistic. The self that is justified is the self at this time and in this place but not the self that has any duration and growth." Heurwas is seeking to acknowledge *maturation* as both a responsibility of the person and a gift of God. With careful reflection on Calvin and Wesley, he encourages us to see that obedience at specific moments is not enough. We must see ourselves as agents in every moment. We can then utilize appropriate psychologies to help us understand some of the specific tasks and issues in our developmental growth.

Reflection

Three dimensions, then, are involved in our development of a style of pastoral care that is cognizant of development in human beings: the reality of critical moments in life, the reality of God's valuing us at each and every moment in time, and the reality that we are developing creatures in need of perceiving our gifts and responsibilities. Conversion, justification, and sanctification are three highly influential, *living* theological explanations of the developmental capacities of us all.

As with our views of human goodness, these assumptions about developmental capacity are influential in the way we extend pastoral care to others. Excessive devotion to one can lead to distortion in our perception.

As an exercise in examining your own assumptions, keep a journal of the visits you make as a pastor, or the caring you extend in any relationship. Write a verbatim so that you can look at your overall pattern of caring and specific expressions of it. Are there particular kinds of events that compel you to go? What are they? Do you go only in crisis, or is there a routine pattern of checking in with persons whether there is a crisis or not? Are there combinations of these or others that occur? What happens in the conversation? Do you steer the conversation to particular issues, follow wherever the person leads, seek to offer solutions, seek to give reassurance? What do you find that you were doing as compared to what you intended to do? Write down your observations of yourself, and we will have an occasion to inspect them later from other frames of reference.

THE RESPONSIVE CAPACITY
OF HUMAN BEINGS

To be in relationship is to be in the constant act of "responding" to each other. The term "responsive" points out that we are not people who are always in the act of "initiating" something. If that were the case, we would be isolated most of the time. Isolation is a common enough experience because of our distorted convictions that we must be in control or be controlled. But even though our sinfulness leads us into these experiences of isolation with regularity, we are also capable of being responsive to each other. Reaction is one of our gifts. And so we must examine our assumptions again. What do you believe about the capacity we have to be responsive to each other in a genuine way? And how does that assumption affect what you expect of yourself and others?

It may seem all too obvious or too simple to say that we are responsive creatures. But that must be said in order to move on to a discussion of the importance that we attribute to that characteristic. Are relationships something to be utilized "only when needed," with the assumption that the more independent we are the "better" we are? Or are relationships to be viewed as things to be nurtured and developed with constancy? And if we believe the latter, what is the purpose? To be sure we are taken care of? To live out a sense of its being important for us to care for others?

Our Responsiveness and Our Capacity

The orders of creation in the book of Genesis aid us in understanding our capacity to respond and its purpose. In Genesis 2, verse 18 reports that God said, "It is not good that the man should be alone; I will make him a helper fit for him." Note that "aloneness" is not viewed as the healthy or desirable state for man, or humanity. The solution is, of course, a relationship. That relationship has very specific characteristics, which are caught up in the meaning of the word translated "fit." The Hebrew word conveys that this helper is to be held in equal regard, valued to the same degree, and not to be viewed as subordinate. Furthermore, the partner or "helper" is capable of responding to the formerly isolated man. The solution to the aloneness is more than physical company. There is capacity to be responsive, to share, to be involved with, indeed to reflect to the man who he really is. While that reference is to the male/ female relationship in specific, it is appropriate to generalize and point this out as an intention for all relationships. Other human beings are here as a gift to save us from aloneness, to enable us to understand ourselves more effectively and to contribute in a significant way to the understanding and development of others. Further reflection on this theme, with accompanying study of Scripture and theology, can be a helpful procedure in your development of an understanding of the nature and function of pastoral care.

Our Responsiveness and Our Need

A second observation serves as a partial explanation of the *need* for this emphasis on responsiveness. In our discussion of finitude and sin it was noted that we are, by nature, dependent creatures, prone to distort a proper understanding of who we are. There is the need. Relationships with other persons offer a *partial* corrective for those limitations. They are partial in that we are relying on other persons who also experience limitations and pet distortions, but they and we also possess certain levels of insight which can add to the understanding that we already have. Such relationships provide the warmth of company, the insight to help us grow, the support we need in difficult tasks, and the jolt that is important to break through our distortions. They bring a greater sense of completeness to us in our state of incompleteness.

Under this second observation, then, lies the importance of viewing our capacity to respond as a *serving quality.* Remember that the description from the passage in Genesis first speaks of the partner as a helper. "Servant" would even be a proper inference, if we look at the import carefully. For one to need a servant is to say that one is not complete. Servant in this context is not a mere luxury. It is a necessity. Without the helper, the person's survival, in the richest meaning of the word, is at stake.

My colleague James Mays has astutely pointed out the import of this suggestion many places in Scripture. It is done in a way that may not be very satisfactory to men or women, as he notes. The role of Jesus frequently is one of servant. Those were the most difficult expressions of himself for the disciples to accept. To have their feet washed by their master! Frequently the disciples, men, are chided by their master for their desire to exercise power. Women are frequently commended by him for their recognition of the importance of so-called weaker, and serving, acts.

The message here is not one of sexual stereotyping but a clear emphasis on the importance of service as a necessary vehicle to being human. We are served, and we serve in relationships. And so it is that we can say that we *need* to be in relationship, in order to serve and enrich each other.

Our Responsiveness and the Church

The church is, of course, the concrete theological expression of community. In it we find relationships available. In it we are nurtured. In it we find comfort and relief in times of stress. In it we find the opportunity to serve.

The church is a concrete expression of God's design to "see to it" that we not live out our lives in isolation. We have already noted the tendency, because of our sin, to isolate ourselves and avoid the claims and calls to freedom. Certainly that experience occurs within the church. Yet, in the experience of being known by others, both human and divine, we are invited again and again, in the context of the church, to know ourselves and to serve.

The doctrines of the communion of saints and the priesthood of all believers are claims that we are all "in it together." We are free to be responsive in the church rather than enslaved to an isolation from it. The invitation is always there. It is in that community, living under the realities of commonality and necessity, experiencing the freeing and visionary dimensions of God's grace, that we are empowered to live out what it means to be authentically human in whatever ways we can. A community of faith calls us out of isolation and self-preoccupation into the experience of caring for others and allowing ourselves to be cared for. There we can affirm our dependency as strength. It also calls us out of a frenetic avoidance of self into a responsible and continuing examination of self, nurturing the image in which we were created.

Reflection

Consider again your assumptions about the capacity and nature of our responsiveness, or relatedness, to one another as human beings. Take some time to examine your own expectations of a relationship. What do you want? Take some time as well to talk to other persons about what they expect and hope for. Watch carefully for descriptive words that give a clue to those expectations. Does the person find relationships "a lot of trouble," "something I can't get along without," "a necessity when I'm having problems," "something to be endured"? Are there more positive affirmations, such as "a source of strength," "something which I work hard to place a priority on," "my source of support in joy and in sorrow"? Whatever you believe, fundamentally, about our capacity to respond and the purpose of that capacity will color your style of caring in very distinct ways.

GOD'S ACTIVITY WITH HUMAN BEINGS

Discussions of the goodness, development, and responsiveness of human beings are an examination of God's creation. Now we come to a discussion of God's interaction with his creation. Our thesis is that the assumptions we hold about this arena, too, affect our style of pastoral care.

Grace is one of the most important frames of reference within which we discuss God's involvement with us. Two of the most prominent manifestations of that grace are in his initiative and his faithfulness to us. There are two perspectives from which we shall view them. The first is with regard to the way in which God's grace seems to manifest itself. The second will be the effects of that manifestation.

The Form of God's Grace

First, God's grace comes to us freely and without dependence on our asking for it or earning it. This is part of the radical nature of God's involvement in our lives. Contrary to most views of the way in which one goes about getting something, God refuses to "buy into" such a system. Several implications are to be drawn from this first affirmation.

Primarily, the notion of God's grace coming freely means that there is no control that we can exert upon the coming of God into our lives. It is his initiative, not ours. His grace appears when we do not deserve it and when we do not expect it. It also appears when, at least in our eyes, we do deserve it. It also appears and is experienced by some who do expect it, and we may find ourselves enraged that some individuals could so glibly "count on it" during tough times and seem to have their belief come true! So, God's grace is infuriating, awe-inspiring, and life-giving in its unpredictability and evasion of our best efforts to "manage it." A captivating illustration of belief in God's free exercise of his grace is the comment of a small businessman that whenever a big decision was made in his company, all employees from the janitors up participated. When asked the reason for the practice, he replied that he had learned from his belief in the Holy Spirit that you never know where the next good idea may come from. In like fashion, God's grace does appear at any time, in any form, and we never know.

A second component of the character of God's grace revolves around the notion of constancy. While we speak of grace as if it comes and goes, our belief is that it is always there. We often speak of it as faithfulness. A helpful comparison can be made with the experience of our own caring for someone. While *we* know that we care on a relatively constant basis, the other person experiences that caring from us in more scattered fashion. There are moments in the ongoing experience of a relationship when the other person is more aware of our care than others. That is true, not only because of the person's own changing awareness and responsiveness to our care but also because we are more visible and intentional in our expression of that caring in some moments than in others. The scattered moments in which the care comes through more clearly are crucial to the knowledge and trust that develop in the person for whom we care. Similarly, in any relationship in which we know that we are cared for, we can best describe it by referring to specific events in which that care came through more clearly. Those events convinced us of the reality of that caring on a constant basis.

So is the case with God's grace. Particular events in our heritage and our personal history stand out to us as evidence that God's grace is real and constant. It is both unpredictable in our experience of it and predictable in our belief in it. It is both gratifying and infuriating in its availability that is beyond our control.

The Effect of God's Grace

The effect of God's grace is one of giving us vision, freeing us to respond, and inviting us into relationship with him and other persons so that we may come to terms with our limits, our gifts, and our capacities to be most human.

The ingredients of this perspective are important. First, there is freedom rather than enslavement. God's grace does not force upon us a style that is impossible or in opposition to our identity or inner core of experience. Rather, we are given vision to see more of our identity and inner reservoir of promise. Martin Marty has written a delightfully helpful little book, entitled *You Are Promise,* in which he points out that we are of value and worth *now.* That discovery frees us both to be and to become rather than disparaging our present self in quest of who we shall be. That is an effect of God's grace. It frees us because the grace and power are present now, rather than some time later. The promise is not all in the future. It is here, now, in God's grace. That is part of the content of the grace being unearned. It is free, and that frees us, right now.

A second ingredient of the effect of God's grace involves the content of the freedom. We are freed to look at ourselves in terms of both limits and gifts. Freedom is not freedom if it consists merely of optimistic euphoria about my potential. To be unaware of my limitations is to be trapped or enslaved by them. The result of such blindness would be to have them creeping up on me continuously and unpredictably, unavailable for correction or discipline. My limitations are an essential ingredient of my self, and to deny them would be to deny who I am, compelling me to live a life of falsehood and segmentation, experiencing myself only partially. By God's grace I receive the opportunity to look at my limitations and live with them knowledgeably and freely rather than ignoring them compulsively and blindly. The courage to do that comes not from me but from the knowledge that the limitations are known and acknowledged by another and thus become speakable to me as well.

Acknowledgment of limits also frees me to look at and "own" my gifts. To live with my limitations without the experience of being known in them would leave me guilty and ashamed and isolated, unable to lay claim to the strengths that are also mine. The effect of God's grace is to free me from being enslaved by the guilt and shame, giving me the freedom and ability to claim and live out my strengths as well as my weaknesses, freeing me to depend upon that grace rather than on myself alone. It is because of this reality that the phrase "in need of God's grace" should follow any statement about human nature, be it complimentary or derogatory. Without that grace we would not perceive either the limitations or the gifts clearly because of the distortion of sin that would emphasize one or the other. God's grace, then, has the effect of "empowering us" to see ourselves as we are. His grace enables us to live out our lives with moments of real integrity. Our experience and vision of this reality and power come and go, but the constancy of the grace is there.

Reflection

Write a verbatim or clinical case study of a recent conversation in which you function as a minister, as a member of the priesthood of all believers. As you look over what was said and the impressions you had, avoid evaluating the individual responses for a moment and answer the following questions:

1. What limits were you conscious of in yourself, the other person, and in the conversation generally?
2. What special gifts did you seem to bring, and what gifts do you view the other person to have carried?
3. Where did distortion seem to occur in the conversation?
4. How much hope did you experience? What seems possible as a result of your encounter?
5. Wherein did you have a sense of God's grace?
6. What sort of development do you see occurring with each of you in the relationship generally?

To reflect on questions such as these *before* evaluating specific responses is an important enterprise. Only then have we really inspected the criteria we use in judging effectiveness, discriminating between getting something to happen and having cared in a manner that is faithful to our theological beliefs.

For Further Reading

Brueggemann, Walter. *The Prophetic Imagination.* Fortress Press, 1978.
Buber, Martin. *I and Thou.* Charles Scribner's Sons, 1970.
Cobb, John. *Theology and Pastoral Care.* Fortress Press, 1977.

Heurwas, Stanley. *Character and the Christian Life.* Trinity University Press, 1975.

Hiltner, Seward. *Theological Dynamics.* Abingdon Press, 1972.

Interpretation, Vol. 33 (Spring 1979).

Kierkegaard, Søren. *The Sickness Unto Death.* Princeton University Press, 1941.

McIntosh, Ian F. *Pastoral Care and Pastoral Theology.* Westminster Press, 1972.

Marty, Martin E. *You Are Promise.* Argus Communications, 1973.

Mayeroff, Milton. *On Caring.* Harper & Row, 1971.

Mays, James L. ". . . And She Served Them," *As I See It,* Vol. IX, No. 2 (Nov. 1978).

Moltmann, Jürgen. *Man: Christian Anthropology in the Conflicts of the Present.* Fortress Press, 1974.

Niebuhr, Reinhold. *The Nature and Destiny of Man.* 2 vols. Charles Scribner's Sons, 1941–43.

Oates, Wayne E. *Christ and Selfhood.* Association Press, 1961.

———. *On Becoming Children of God.* Westminster Press, 1969.

Oglesby, Wm. B., Jr. *Biblical Themes for Pastoral Care.* Abingdon Press, 1980.

———. "Pastoral Care and Counseling in Biblical Perspective," *Interpretation,* Vol. 27 (July 1973).

Oglesby, Wm. B., Jr., ed. *The New Shape of Pastoral Theology: Essays in Honor of Seward Hiltner.* Abingdon Press, 1969.

Pannenberg, Wolfhart. *What Is Man?* Fortress Press, 1970.

Thornton, Edward E. *Theology and Pastoral Counseling.* Prentice-Hall, 1964.

Williams, Daniel Day. *The Minister and the Care of Souls.* Harper & Row, 1977.

2

Principles That Give Integrity to Pastoral Care

Our theological ground can be used to formulate a particular style of caring. The derived principles provide a standard by which care can be designed and evaluated.

"Integrity" is a defining criterion for the selection of principles. A part of the meaning of the term is caught up in the word "consistency." Is a given principle consistent with our views on God's manner of involvement with us? The principles should reflect the assumptions or beliefs discussed in Chapter 1, if they are to lend integrity to pastoral care.

A second part of the meaning of integrity is a sense of "having done enough." Does the principle embody an *action* that is consistent with our theology? We are people who not only believe but act. Integrity carries that sense of doing as well as believing.

Erik Erikson, an intensely provocative psychologist and writer, speaks of old age in terms of "integrity versus despair" *(Identity and the Life Cycle)*. A person looks back over her or his life and evaluates it in terms of whether enough was done. Certainly everything that might have been done did not take place, but the criterion is the sense of having done "enough." That is integrity.

Principles developed here are derived in terms of their

consistency with our theological assumptions. Further, they reflect an emphasis on describing the action that is enough for the pastor who is seeking to be faithful in his or her caring.

INITIATIVE

Our principles begin where the pastoral relationship begins, with an action on the part of one person. The action is one of reaching out. Pastoral initiative presumes that it is important and appropriate for the pastor, the caring person, to reach out, even if uninvited. The principle, to have integrity, must take into account our theological assumptions about the nature of human beings and the nature of God. Helping theories raise questions about the issue of initiative. Assumptions are made about the ability or likelihood of a person's reaching out for help. An optimistic belief about perception and courage will assume that people see and ask for help when they need it.

Initiative and Human Nature

The theological assumptions advanced in Chapter 1 raise questions about the ability or the willingness of a person to reach out during a time of distress. Human limitations, the distortions in perception, the failure to recognize gifts and abilities, and the tendency to isolate oneself out of pride or shame are troublesome. Those realities move against a naive assumption that we can blissfully sit in an office and expect persons in need of help to appear at our doorstep. Initiative means going to them. It is based on the hard-nosed belief that people don't always know when they need help. And if they do know, they may not have the courage to admit it.

Crisis periods are not the only time when it is valuable to initiate pastoral care. Our understanding of human beings as developing creatures lends importance to making regular contacts with people to "get to know them" apart from some dramatic event. In fact, people in crisis are more receptive to help if initiative has been taken toward them long before the crisis occurs. Relationships must have *developed* in order for people to make the most productive use of pastoral care in a crisis. And the initiative in forming that relationship must often be exercised by the pastoral person.

Failure to exercise initiative often is a reflection of our own human condition. We fail to perceive or are fearful of offending. Because of *our* distortion, we do not perceive that a person is in need of help. The result is a missed opportunity for both to experience commonality in caring when it is sorely needed.

Initiative and God's Grace

The principle of initiative is consistent with our view of human nature. It is also consistent with our view of God's relationship to us, a relationship initiated by him. God's grace is neither dependent on our asking for it nor dependent on the way in which we respond. It gives something without the demand of getting something in return. It alerts us to the perception that we matter and that we are not alone. It teaches us that we can grow best in an experience of community.

Initiative in Action

Initiative is not usually a dramatic act. It is unusual in a world that values privacy and would be described by some as "sticking your nose into other people's business." Another, and more hopeful, description of it is as an act of telling people what you see and care about. The only difference between those two descriptions is in the perception, not in the act itself. For instance, to go to the home of a parishioner who has not appeared at church for some time should be done out of a desire to express interest and caring. It is to be hoped that your visit will be perceived that way by the parishioner. But it may be seen as a manipulative attempt on your part to get your parishioner back to church *and no more!* You have no control over the response. You do have control over your exercise of the caring. The principle of initiative calls for the expression of care regardless of what the response to it may be!

Physical action is certainly one implication of the principle of initiative. Regular visitation stands as the cardinal expression of a caring process that is distinctively pastoral. Going whenever you hear of death, illness, relationship problems, etc., is crucial. If the homework has been done in terms of ongoing visitation, you are more likely to hear of the legitimate crises.

Initiative as "Observing"

More than physically showing up is involved. Initiative also implies telling people what you see. The pastor is an observer. On the assumption that people's perception is often impaired, one task of initiative is to tell people what we see. On the assumption that often we too are limited and distorting creatures, we make our observations in a way that leaves room for our being corrected. Proper expression of initiative allows room for everyone in the relationship to grow.

James Dittes, in his helpful book *The Church in the Way,* tells the delightful incident of an usher who always counted the members at worship during the morning prayer. The pastor had come to expect the clicking of the counter as he said, "Our Father . . ." Finally, the pastor took initiative in the form of wondering out loud about why the usher chose that particular point in the service to do that job. An observation was advanced, instead of a complaint. The result was the usher's confession of deep discomfort with prayer and a decision to sit down with the pastor to talk about it.

When a couple who have always been seen together in church begin to come separately, that can be an occasion to observe that you have noticed the change and wondered what it meant. When the church grapevine keeps saying that good old George seems awfully depressed lately, you can exercise initiative by going to good old George to say that you have heard that he seems down in the dumps and wonder if that is so. Both the couple and George have the opportunity to clarify in response to that kind of initiative.

We must be careful, in exercising initiative, not to presume to know more than we do. We too are finite and prone to see potential divorce in normal conflict, anger in a decision to skip church one Sunday, or depression in a perfectly understandable attempt to get some privacy. We are prone to move in with power instead of grace. To guard against that tendency, it is important to exercise our initiative in a way that says, "I notice that . . ." and "I care." The form of God's grace that we seek to embody describes a condition and invites, not demands, us to respond.

Certainly there is risk in taking initiative such as I have described. In premarital counseling sessions I have had the experience of saying to a couple, "I'm disturbed by the way in which you two don't seem to know each other very well or for very long." In one case the couple stalked out and down the street to a justice of the peace, who "wouldn't get so personal." In response to the same kind of observation, another couple looked at each other, breathed a sigh of relief, and said, "Let's postpone this wedding until we decide whether we really want to get married." Initiative on my part was responded to in very different ways, but in both cases I had been consistent in reflecting my high regard for marriage and my having done enough to communicate that serious regard to them. I'll never know whether I was right or wrong in the first case, but I have my prejudice! In both cases, however, the exercise of initiative and the careful shaping of its form was important in order to be faithful to my theological beliefs and to them as persons created in the image of God.

The principle of initiative in pastoral care is *necessary* to be consistent with our beliefs about human nature and God's involvement with us. The exercise of it is *reflective* of God's grace. There is belief and action. Both must be exercised if we are to care with integrity.

FAITHFULNESS

Caring necessarily means a relationship. The principle of initiative provides definition for the pastor's responsibility in beginning the relationship. That beginning may take place through the physical act of going, uninvited, to a person. Responding to a request for help or attention by directing the conversation to the important issues is another exercise of initiative. The principle of faithfulness further defines the form which the pastoral relationship takes, once initiated.

Models for the exercise of faithfulness are to be found throughout Scripture. God's faithfulness to Israel, the keeping of the covenant, Hosea's faithfulness to Gomer, the frequent references to marriage as paradigmatic to God's faithfulness, the death and resurrection of Jesus—all characterize for us the content of faithfulness. A demanding principle, it distinctively illustrates what it means to care in a pastoral manner.

Faithfulness and Presence

To be faithful to someone is to stay with that person. Physical and emotional commitment play a part. In caring for you in a faithful manner, I promise to be both physically available and emotionally involved. Both are not possible

all the time, but the commitment is to maintain that faithfulness as an intention. Note that the commitment is to *be* a
particular way. Period. No expectations are placed on the
recipients of the care. They do not have to behave or feel
in particular ways to keep the care coming. Faithfulness is
covenantal rather than contractual. I make a covenant to be
faithful, to stay with you. A contract would stipulate what
you must do in order to "force" me to continue my promised behavior.

The linkage of faithfulness to initiative is readily evident.
I come to you without demanding a response. I remain with
you without demanding a response. Reflective of God's
grace, the principle of faithfulness is a promise. The promise
is one of availability and willingness to give attention to the
person, who deserves such availability and attention because she or he is God's creature—no more and no less.

Presence as an expression of faithfulness will be exercised
in various ways. Implied already, the caring goes on *without
dependence on results.* Pastoral visitation of the sick, for example, goes on even if the patient doesn't get well. A covenant
continues. The pastor visits the sick. Period. No demand is
made that the patient make pleasant conversation, express
gratitude, or increase a pledge to the church. The same
should be true of regular pastoral visitation in the congregation. The pastor will come calling for no reason other than
being faithful. Other images of the pastor as visiting *only* in
time of trouble have caused great distress. I well recall my
father, who is a minister, telling of his stop at the office of
one of his parishioners. The intention was to invite him to
lunch—a simple visit. The man's secretary was alarmed at
my father's presence and rushed her boss out of a meeting
with the news that something terrible must have happened
because the minister had come! The exercise of faithfulness
can eventually put such fears to rest. There need be no
special condition to make a person deserving of the pastor's

visit. He or she comes out of the promise, the covenant, to be faithful and thus present in the lives of the members of a congregation.

Presence is further exercised through the discipline of *listening.* One of the greatest experiences of being cared for is the knowledge that someone will remain with us and hear us. It is a welcome contrast to the age of information and advice in which we live. All too often we pay the price of listening to advice just to have the experience of someone listening to us first.

A most impressive teacher on listening as an expression of faithfulness was a hospital patient. She had come to deliver her child. Her baby was born dead. She called for a chaplain, and I happened to be available. When I walked into the room, she didn't ask my name. She just began talking. She talked about her hopes and dreams of motherhood, of her not understanding why this had happened to her, of her anger toward God for letting it happen, and finally of her plans for the future. I never got in a word. When she finished, she said, "Thank you for all your help," rolled over and went to sleep. I left asking what I had done. Now I know. I had listened without interrupting her. I had been faithful to her instead of to myself. My preference, out of my own nervousness, would have been to interrupt her and talk so that I wouldn't have to listen. But to be truly present to her, my gift was keeping my mouth shut.

That faithful act of listening is a gift the pastor has to offer. We can often be far more articulate about our concerns if we know that the other person isn't champing at the bit, waiting for us to take a breath so that he or she can tell us what to do. Such listening is indeed a gift. In the next chapter we shall discuss prayer as one of the resources we have to offer as an experience of being heard.

Presence is not always an easy or pleasurable expression of faithfulness. In fact, it can often be taken advantage of.

There are many people who will take us quite literally in the expectation that we be available *all the time*. So, we must define our presence with words and actions that provide more definition to the meaning of faithfulness.

Faithfulness and Promises

Our understanding of faithfulness as presence is further refined by the additional element of keeping promises. The promises we make become effective teaching devices as they shape expectations and set limits.

Judgments on our faithfulness often hinge on the promises we make. As we leave a nursing home, the casual promise we make to come back next week becomes something concrete for the person to depend upon. If our promise carries with it an unspoken "maybe," then someone will be sorely disappointed. The grief-stricken widow may hang on to the promises we make about how long the pain will last. We had best be careful about making promises to her or to a husband who demands a guarantee that marriage counseling will "really help."

What do we promise? Well, we promise to be faithful, for one thing. We promise to be available, but how available? Limits must be set on those promises. I remember a phone call that came to a pastor while I was in his home. His end of the conversation was all that could be heard. "Hello . . . Yes. I told you that I would only talk to you about that in our regular meeting on Wednesday afternoons . . . No, I won't talk to you now. Good-by." My first reaction was one of anger toward the minister for being so blunt and ungracious to whoever had made that call. Then I learned that this was an emotionally handicapped adolescent who had become very dependent on him. There had been constant phone calls, bids for attention, visits to his office at the church. Necessarily, he had set limits on these contacts, telling her that he would meet *faithfully* every week on Wednesday afternoon. Other visits or conversations were strictly forbidden. She was learning *how* she could depend on him. He was setting limits to enable her to learn and to enable him to carry out the many other responsibilities he had. Promises made, limits set—they go hand in hand.

No list of acceptable and unacceptable promises would be appropriate here. The point is that promises are important. Promises not made are equally important. All are testimony to our faithfulness.

Promises, as presence, must take into account our beliefs about our nature and God's nature. We are limited and cannot be eternally present, nor can we make and keep too many promises. God's promises are ones of faithfulness, and there are limits to them. Study of Scripture and theology will strengthen us in our reflection and strategy for being faithful. We may need to examine our willingness to come to grips with our limits. We may need to look further at our own level of acceptance of God's promises. There just may be dissatisfaction with the way he set it up and a distorted attempt on our part to "run the world better." Such subtle temptations will bring us to terms with our limits quickly, or they will detract from an exercise of faithfulness that reflects theological integrity.

Faithfulness and Freedom

How much, we ask in great theological debates, are we free to respond to God's grace? And how much are we "unable to resist" when that grace comes to us? Those same questions occur in quite practical ways in pastoral relationships.

Being present is one important expression of faithfulness. Promises are another. But what about the freedom of the person for whom we care? Does she or he have the freedom to say "No!"? If we are resisted in our good efforts, do we continue to stand at the door and knock, or even consider beating it down?

The reality of finitude, sin, the developmental character of human beings, and the reality of God's grace confront us again. People do say no to offers of help, and they may indeed be unable or unwilling to recognize their need for the help they refuse. The time may not be right. On the other hand, since we are human beings also, we may have perceived a need incorrectly. Their "no" is instructive to us, and we may learn from it. The time may not be right for us to be able to perceive correctly. Either or both of us, pastor and parishioner, may need to grow before caring can take place in a concrete way, if at all.

Some people may be willing to get help but *not from us!* They don't like us. They prefer to talk with someone else. Our faithfulness at that point is to make a referral. Our faithfulness acknowledges their freedom not to receive care from us. Equally important, we may not like some people, finding ourselves unwilling to work with them. The freedom is there for us to make a referral, doing it in as caring a manner as possible. *We cannot take care of everyone,* but we can be faithful to them by exercising our freedom to get them help in a way that is responsible to them and to ourselves.

Also involved with freedom are frequency and duration of our presence and promises. A man or a woman may be grateful to us, but may also need time away from us. In fact, too much presence may communicate that we don't believe they are able to get along without us. The necessity for freedom includes the importance of privacy. Henri Nouwen, in his book *The Living Reminder,* speaks of the "ministry of absence" in a compelling way. Our absence gives persons freedom to discover the abilities that accompany their limits. It further gives the pastor opportunity to exercise other ministries on the person's behalf, such as study, prayer, rallying other people to their support.

Invitation has become an important concept for me in trying to understand the place of freedom in the principle of faithfulness. Pastoral care involves the issuing of an invitation to people. The invitation is based on observations we have made. It is also based on our belief that God's grace comes with constancy and is always available. We don't have to respond to an invitation at one particular moment out of fear that it will never return.

To "invite" persons to receive care acknowledges their freedom to refuse. They are seen as developing beings for whom the time may not be right for help. Further, our perception may be wrong, and our approach of invitation is as much an inquiry as it is an assertion. To demand, rather than invite, would deny those theological beliefs we hold about human nature. To be faithful, we must acknowledge freedom.

Faithfulness and Disciplined Progress

Implicit in what has been said about faithfulness is a demand for rigor. It is not easy to be faithful. Undertaking pastoral care with integrity requires that one be disciplined. Caring is a process and not a scattered array of unrelated events. Faithfulness as a disciplined process occurs in at least four areas.

The first is *study.* To be faithful, a pastor must regularly study Scripture and theology and use them in disciplined reflection about the exercise of ministry. Along with that must come observation of human nature. Such study means regular interaction with people *accompanied* by later reflection. We must learn from that interaction, not just experience it. Along with the study of people is the study of ourselves. Introspection is essential in our effort to understand the caring process. Time for prayer and private meditation, as well as self-inspecting conversations with trusted others, is an important discipline *if* we are to care for others in a manner that is distinctively pastoral.

Disciplined progress, secondly, involves *good management.* We cannot be faithful in a haphazard manner. Study of human nature and self will reveal issues in need of regular attention in the life of a congregation and a community. Careful administration will see to it that we are faithful to our discoveries. If we believe that the grief process extends beyond the funeral, for instance, then we devise a plan of pastoral care to ensure that we regularly visit the bereaved. Without such a plan, more immediately visible events will lead us to forget that person sitting, quietly depressed, at home. If we believe that regular visitation builds up trust and caring possibilities for the future, then we had better devise a plan to see to it that visitation takes place. Faithfulness demands planning.

Third, many occasions of caring call for more *formal counseling* on a regular basis. Knowledge about developing relationships will enable us to direct counseling in a positive manner. We must be disciplined in how much formal counseling we take on at any given time, and what we expect of it. Study is called for again. Reflection on where the relationship has gone, willingness to recognize how our own feelings affect that process, and awareness of the other person's feelings for us are crucial if we are to be faithful in a manner that has integrity.

Fourth, faithfulness involves *teaching* people. The pastoral function is tied closely, in Ephesians 4, for instance, to the teaching function. While our involvement with persons involves a great deal of listening and understanding, it also involves teaching them some things about themselves, about relationships, about human nature, and about the formation of character. Our study is crucial because we will ᴜe teachers when we function as pastors, whether in a routine encounter, a crisis intervention, or in formal, ongoing counseling. To be a teacher requires discipline and awareness that learning takes place *over time.*

FOR YOUR REFLECTION

These principles are more than theories. They are principles for *practice.* So, take a moment to check on your exercise of them. Write a verbatim. It is a time-honored learning tool in pastoral care.

Now, for your evaluation, look at what you have said and done. Evaluate yourself in terms of each of the characteristics of the two principles in this chapter. For example, where did the initiative for your conversation come from? Was any initiative exercised in the conversation to focus the concerns? Did you make any observations about what you saw and heard? How would you evaluate your faithfulness? Did you provide verbal or nonverbal assurance about your interest and intent to "stick with" your parishioners in some way? Did you allow them freedom to avoid issues that you felt should be dealt with? Did you listen, or did you tend to decide what they needed to do and tell them? Did you teach them anything?

For Further Reading

Clinebell, Howard J., Jr. *Basic Types of Pastoral Counseling.* Abingdon Press, 1966.

Dittes, James E. *The Church in the Way.* Charles Scribner's Sons, 1967.

Gerkin, Charles V. *Crisis Experience in Modern Life: Theory and Theology in Pastoral Care.* Abingdon Press, 1979.

Hiltner, Seward. *The Christian Shepherd: Some Aspects of Pastoral Care.* Abingdon Press, 1959.

———. *Preface to Pastoral Theology.* Abingdon Press, 1958.

Hiltner, Seward, and Colston, Lowell. *The Context of Pastoral Counseling.* Abingdon Press, 1961.

McNeill, John T. *A History of the Cure of Souls.* Harper & Row, 1977.

Nouwen, Henri J. *The Living Reminder.* Seabury Press, 1977.

Oates, Wayne E. *The Christian Pastor,* Revised and Enlarged. Westminster Press, 1980.

———. *Pastoral Counseling.* Westminster Press, 1974.

Oates, Wayne E., and Neely, Kirk H. *Where to Go for Help,* Revised and Enlarged Edition. Westminster Press, 1972.

Oglesby, Wm. B., Jr. *Referral in Pastoral Counseling.* Abingdon Press, 1978.

3
Theological Resources for Times of Caring

Beliefs and principles, as outlined in the first two chapters, naturally lead toward conviction and acts to live out those beliefs. Both religious and psychological resources are available to us, and ministers often become "translators" in the dialogue between the two. It is important that we understand both languages in the interest of serving the whole person. This chapter will illustrate some of the theological resources at our disposal.

Several books have appeared in recent years calling us back to proper use of the theological, or spiritual, disciplines in the practice of pastoral care. Two of the more helpful have been *The Minister as Diagnostician,* by Paul Pruyser, and *The Moral Context of Pastoral Care,* by Don Browning. They are recommended to you for further reading in this area.

REPENTANCE

To "repent of one's sins" has deep roots in the Judeo-Christian tradition. The literal meaning of the word "repentance" is a "turning back" as a result of a "change of mind." Repentance involves a perception, an acknowledgment, that a condition or action needs to be changed. Old

Testament prophets spoke of repentance in terms of the negative—a perception that something is wrong. Turning away is the response to that perception.

Repentance is not the popularly stereotyped "guilt trip." Three components are included in the process: (1) the realization or acknowledgment of a particular condition or action, (2) a sincere expression of regret and willingness to take responsibility for whatever has been done—taking the consequences, (3) the decision to change. These three constitute a process of reorientation.

A call to repent is an open confession that we are limited creatures with a tendency to distort our limitations to our own self-interests. Repentance enables us to claim what is possible for us as creatures who are also gifted and prone to live best when in community. It is only when we have opportunity to admit to the mistakes, the occasions of falling short, also known as sin, that we have the opportunity to realize what more we can be.

Repentance is never called for without the promise of forgiveness. New Testament writers note that repentance in the deepest sense is beyond human powers. It is both demanded and given. To exercise repentance without the hope of forgiveness is a distorted expression of repentance. We certainly see persons who seem to be preoccupied with calling attention to the numerous wrong acts they have committed. Being forgiven does not seem to have occurred to them, nor does it seem important. Rather, the objective appears to be an experience of feeling bad in and of itself. The theological objective of repentance, however, is to lay the ground for the experience of forgiveness. Only that use of repentance should be borne in mind when encouraging or participating in it in our exercise of pastoral care.

Repentance, then, is carried out in a context that "expects" something else. More than a simple recitation of wrongdoing, it is perception of reality, assumption of responsibility, and commitment to renewal in the deepest personal and corporate sense. The context we set for such an experience may cooperate with that process, or interfere with it. Therefore, we must be familiar with its crucial dynamics, one of which is guilt.

Repentance and Guilt

Acknowledgment and assumption of responsibility are the components of guilt, understood in a theological sense. Multiple frames of reference, theological and psychological, distinguish between factual guilt and experiential guilt, objective and subjective, true and false. The distinctions point out the tendency many persons have to claim guilt when not guilty, or exaggeration of guilt beyond the dimensions that are appropriate to the act. Further observation reminds us that one does not necessarily have to be guilty to feel guilty. Or, conversely, one does not automatically feel guilty when actually guilty.

Repentance, to be used with theological validity in pastoral care, must deal with guilt that has certain features. First, there must be an identifiable act or condition, for which the person is, in deed and in fact, guilty. *Or,* there must be some clear standards or expectations which the person has violated or failed to live up to. With both acts and standards, there must be some generally verifiable code within a community to which the person has sought to subscribe. All of this is to say that guilt is carried within the context of relationships, a community. Behavior for which one repents is behavior that affects people and/or the general welfare of the community, including but not limited to oneself. This is consonant with our discussion in Chapter 1 about the responsive aspect of human nature. Further, there is an acknowledgment on the part of the person that there are expectations *outside of the self* that are being met. Certainly, a personal moral code is involved, but the relational or community factor in repentance is a corrective for the distortion that may occur in the personal evaluation of self. If the guilt arises from distorted perception, repentance is not the appropriate resource.

If the above conditions are not met when a person seeks to repent, we may well be dealing with an experience of guilt that is not consonant with repentance. To encourage repentance of acts not committed or to offer forgiveness for guilt not verifiable violates the person. It fails to provide an experience of forgiveness that has integrity. Indeed, it may cover over more serious problems. In such a case, the act of repentance becomes a diversion for the person rather than a potential experience of healing.

Some years ago I received a phone call from a woman I did not know. She called because I was the first minister she had found in the phone book. Her expressed intention was a need to confess a terrible sin about her raising of her child. But first she had a question: "When the Final Judgment comes, will those who are living be judged before those who have already died? Or will those who have already died be judged before those who are currently living?" Further inquiry about the question revealed that her son, when eighteen years old, had impregnated his girl friend, refused to marry her, joined the army and been killed in Vietnam. The mother's aim was to repent of her failure as a mother. What had she done to have her child turn out like that? She was expressing the hope that when God judged the world, she would be in line before her son so that she could atone for his sins, and thus her own.

The example is extreme, but not that atypical of people who will really admit to guilt issues with which they struggle. Most significant, however, was that as I listened to this woman, she moved away from the fear of judgment and the necessity of repentance for herself and her son. The deeper issue was her need to grieve over his death several years ago. Her desperation to "take care of him" had postponed the more significant need to grieve. Too quick an acceptance of the repentance and premature forgiveness would have failed to meet this woman in her real pain. Had the relationship been more than one phone call, she would no doubt have returned to her sense of inadequacy as a mother and an examination of her faithfulness in living according to her moral beliefs. But *first* was the need to acknowledge loss, not guilt.

Ministers hear from many people who, compulsively or mistakenly, come to repent. Parents come searching for "sins" they have committed which may explain a child's handicap. Such feelings are not limited by race, class, sex, or socioeconomic level. People search for guilt to explain what has happened to them. They are not always in need of repentance, even though they may say so. They often are in need of understanding, both emotional and intellectual.

There are those who do need to repent and have something to repent of, however. Children and adults need to say "I'm sorry" to someone. They are guilty of harsh words, physical abuse, competitive instincts that lead them to run over another person, an internal delight that another person's misfortune resulted in their own profit. Like Robert Louis Stevenson's Dr. Jekyll and Mr. Hyde, they try to separate neatly their evil nature from their "good." Admission of the condition is a constructive pursuit of building up the community and the person. Some forms of counseling avoid the acceptance of an expression of guilt, labeling all feelings and actions as "understandable" and thus acceptable. Repentance, in our theological view, is a real need as well as a ritual. To listen, to understand, to agree, and to offer forgiveness, *in that order,* is to provide a person with hope and a motivation to continue in the development of self, the sanctification process. The repentance will have been real.

An appropriate use of repentance as a theological resource can be seen in the case of a husband who was referred to his minister by a psychiatrist. He had been involved in an affair, felt guilty, and had gone into psychotherapy. Now he understood the reasons, had insight into the personal dynamics that led him into the involvement. He knew ways in which to work on the relationship with his wife in the hope of making it a more enriching relationship for both of them. She did not know of his affair, and he did not intend to tell her. At the same time, he could not bring himself to begin the actual work on enriching the marriage. The referral to the minister was made out of the man's sense of needing to be forgiven for what he had done.

In telling his story again, with tears, he brought the minister up to date on where he had come and said, "But even though I understand why I did it, that doesn't make what I did right, does it?"

> **PASTOR:** Having insight doesn't make the pain of what you did go away.
> **PARISHIONER:** No, because what I did was wrong. Don't you agree that what I did was wrong?
> **PASTOR:** Yes. (Silence)
> **PARISHIONER:** Then what can I do?
> **PASTOR:** You still want to find something to make it okay?
> **PARISHIONER:** No, I want to know whether I can ever forgive myself.
> **PASTOR:** I don't know for sure about that. You have understanding and plans to make up for what you have done, both to you and your wife. The thing I am sure of is that God forgives you, but I don't know whether that will satisfy you or not.
> **PARISHIONER:** I don't know either. But somehow I needed to have someone agree with me that I had done wrong—someone who represented the standards I grew up with. Maybe if I can say I was wrong,

> then I can go to work on the marriage. Just under-
> standing what happened was important, but it wasn't
> enough.

Over a period of time the repentance became real. It was an admission of what happened, which had taken place in psychotherapy in a profitable manner. The additional ingredient of assumption of responsibility—guilt—was necessary for him to move on. The repentance then opened the way for him to experience forgiveness, both his own and that of God, and to reorient himself.

Guilt includes a multitude of meanings in the biblical heritage. Simplest among its definitions is "the state of having missed or failed." Guilt and sin often are interchangeable terms in the Old Testament. Guilt is used in a deeply personal sense, reflecting the power it exercises in the lives of people. To sin may mean to miss, to defy, to do evil intentionally, to deviate from the good, to have contempt for the law, to treat another person unjustly, and to commit many other unseemly acts. The common element in them all is personal *will,* a dimension so personal that a woman or a man is deeply affected by it when it does harm. The personal dimension makes the experience of forgiveness so essential in the process of repentance, so that renewal, or reorientation, may take place.

Repentance and Forgiveness

Forgiveness in the Old Testament is a translation of several words: "wiping away," "removing," and "covering." Priestly in its exercise, forgiveness removes barriers that interfere with relationships and place the person in jeopardy of isolation or wrath. Forgiveness comes primarily as an act of God and secondarily as an act of one person to his or her neighbor. An underlying assumption about forgiveness is that persons cannot live without relationship to God and others. So, forgiveness is necessary to remove those barriers which impede or do away with the possibility of maintaining those crucial relationships. Most intimate of the expressions of what is being sought in the act of forgiveness is the fellowship meal in the Hebrew tradition and the Sacrament of Communion in Christian communities. Forgiveness removes the barriers, renews fellowship, and renews the soul by putting peace in the place of terror and dread.

A second helpful dimension in the concept of forgiveness reveals itself in a Greek word meaning "to be gracious to." Style and manner carry equal importance with results. Graciousness in wiping away the guilt results in a more rapid reorientation. An accusing manner pronounces forgiveness in a way that seems to deny it in the same breath. Graciousness in the assurance of forgiveness makes the covenant to be faithful more real for the recipient, forcing him or her to move on.

Repentance and Pastoral Care

Repentance is an important resource in pastoral care. Opportunity might be a more accurate description of it. In a culture that tends to shy away from fixing blame or assuming responsibility, repentance is an act which does just that. And in the ironic way that appears so often in theology, the very act which is perceived as most to be avoided becomes the process that leads to freedom and renewal. That is what the act of repentance is—a process of renewal.

As pastors, we are perceived as ones who will listen to confessions of wrongdoing and unhappiness. For that reason many persons steer away from us. For that reason many more seek us out, some for less healthy reasons than others. The advantage of this position, if we will use it, is that repentance remains a possibility for people. And our obligation to be faithful applies, regardless of the health of their motivation.

"Acceptance" has been a catchword in much of American culture and counseling circles in recent decades. Unfortunately, the term has come to be understood as an affirmation that there is no wrongdoing. Just "do your own thing." But people do experience a sense of wrongdoing and need to be heard. Repentance is a resource that meets their need and educates them. Confession of wrongdoing does not have to be repetitive self-flagellation. Rather, it is a gracious act when we listen as people expose some of their deepest concerns, helping them to evaluate more carefully, and assuring them that consequences can be borne and reorientation take place. We assure them not only out of our own understanding but out of our belief that we are speaking for a community that regularly affirms forgiveness as a reality in our lives.

Be willing to hear people when they want to repent. Don't forgive them so quickly that they never go through the process. Assist them in "closing the book" on a part of their lives in a way that is responsible and renewing.

PRAYER

Among the traditional resources of the Old and New Testaments, prayer has always been emphatically present. Debate and discomfort occur in many pastoral conversations about the propriety of the use of prayer. All too often the dilemma has been solved by refusing to deal with it and thus failing to use it. No doubt, part of the reason stems from the perception that many people, including ourselves, use it in a magical way. It is the avenue to which we appeal when all else has failed. In other cases, people use it as an avoidance technique. They refuse to discuss an issue, because, they report, they have taken it "to the Lord in prayer." Pastors often resent this most because it takes things out of their hands. They perceive, often correctly, that a person takes things to God in prayer and then excludes the pastor from the conversation.

Of course, we are also familiar with the power that other people can exert over us with an appeal to prayer. For instance, when they are being visited at home or in the hospital, some people may request prayer because they know that it is traditionally the last thing the pastor does before leaving. And they are ready for the pastor to leave!

Prayer as Conversation

We need to remind ourselves and others that prayer is more than a request form. It is an opportunity for us to carry concerns to God in what amounts to a personal conversation about how things are going. Poignantly illustrative are the conversations that occur on the road with Tevye in *Fiddler on the Roof.* As he moves from place to place, he takes the opportunity to tell God how rotten things have been and about the tearful and happy moments in his existence. It is clear that those conversations have been going on for a long time. There seems no doubt in his mind that he has been heard many times.

The conversation is a two-way one. From the conversations reported in Eden between the Lord God and Adam and Eve to the questions Jesus addresses to his Father in the New Testament, we see illustrations of the conversational character of prayer. As a part of the perception that we are limited creatures in need of relationship and community, prayer is a major theological resource for us to "talk it out." We are communicating creatures, not isolation-prone ones. Prayer is resource for us and those for whom we care.

Prayer as Recollection

Prayer is also an instrument to aid us in remembering, which is an important process occurring in conversations with regularity. Talking of something we are concerned about now often leads to our talking about how things went the last time. When Jacob fearfully returns to meet his brother Esau (Genesis 32), he prays in the midst of his anxiety. As he prays about that meeting which is about to take place, he remembers all the things that have led him up to this point in his life. Prayer serves him as a resource for reflection, a remembering process that leads him to make vows about the future because of what he has learned.

Such recollection is crucial in a process of pastoral care. We need to pray about the caring relationships in which we are involved. In that prayer, we may often experience new insight about where we have been and where we are going. It is a resource to be commended at appropriate moments to those for whom we are caring, as well as for ourselves.

Prayer as Discipline

As both conversation and recollection, there is a power in prayer that goes beyond the insights we gain in any other context. And thus it becomes for us an important discipline. Even when we are unconvinced that we are being heard, prayer is important. As in Psalm 22, we are called to cry out, believing in God's faithfulness, even when our experience leads us to think otherwise. That is the point where discipline carries tones of real faithfulness. Do we continue, even when uncertain?

Part of the power that prayer carries as a discipline is the same as that of anything that we do with regularity. It becomes dependable and familiar, thus something to be utilized with comfort. An analogy can be made with physical exercise—it is painful when begun, but there are clearly felt results when it has become a habit. The more comfort and ease we have as we move into prayer, the more power and insight we can gain from it.

But there is more to the power than simply human consistency. We affirm that God is active in the process and often moves us beyond our human limits and distortions when we join in community with him. Prayer is thus a gift when used in disciplined fashion. Through it and God's grace, we experience more of our own gifts that are to be offered in our care of others.

In like fashion, prayer can be commended with integrity to others for whom we care and with whom we live in the community of faith. It then becomes a resource we use and participate in in common, more authentic to our living as human beings.

Prayer as Personal Meditation

Conversation, recollection, and discipline all result in a level of meditation that is important in our living. Henri Nouwen, dealing with prayer in a lecture at the national meeting of the Association for Clinical Pastoral Education in 1976, spoke of the importance of that meditation if we are to care effectively. For instance, he commented, think of the impact it would have for a parishioner to be told that the pastor was unavailable for the day because she or he was praying for the congregation.

Such a procedure would be important for two reasons. First, it is beneficial for the pastor to pray and meditate without interruption on a regular basis. Second, it is beneficial for members of a congregation to know that the pastor believes that he or she is not so essential to their lives that instant availability is necessary. They are in God's hands, not just the pastor's!

Prayer as Community Act

Prayer is not just the private and isolated conversation carried out in a closet. Emphasized time and time again in the Bible and theology, prayer is a corporate act. We come together to pray in formal worship as well as at other more informal times, including a pastoral counseling session, when appropriate. We voice our concerns and gratitude together in corporate prayers of confession, thanksgiving, petition, intercession, and many others. Pastoral care as an expression of community takes prayer seriously and seeks to find ways to use it that are not mechanical but genuine, not compulsive but disciplined, not in desperation but in trust.

HOPE

Hope, from a Judeo-Christian perspective, has a very important definition. It involves looking outside of the self to other resources and promises that can be counted on. Walter Brueggemann describes it as an action—"to live in sure and certain confidence of promises, to function each day trusting that God's promises and purposes will not fail" ("Covenanting as Human Vocation: A Discussion of the Relation of Bible and Pastoral Care," *Interpretation,* Vol. 33, Spring 1979).

To bring hope into the relationship of caring points out that a person has more than self as a resource for living. Acceptance, narrowly conceived, often provides an implicit, if not explicit, expectation that one should look inwardly for help. Hope provides a context and a goal to that experience of acceptance. It says: "Because you are regarded well, you are free to look about you and to rely on resources outside of yourself. Those resources include the other person in this relationship, the community of faith into which you are invited, or of which you are a part, and the grace of God." Hope acknowledges the finitude and sinfulness as real in ourselves and invites us to rely on more certain and dependable resources. At the same time, the resource of hope acknowledges the gifts within ourselves and frees us to use them without a sense of shame and with a sense of commitment to use them well.

So, the pastoral care process, adding hope to the picture,

will say: "Yes, I value you and you are important (acceptance). *But,* you are not all that there is, and you also have
limitations. Let us begin to see who and what you can depend on and lean on in your living." That may mean starting
to look at family more seriously. A search needs to begin for
friendships, for careful involvement in a community, the
church. God's promises—what do they mean? Learning to
live without exclusive reliance on the self—that is the addition that hope makes. And it changes hope from a maneuver
of desperation to an integral part of daily living.

The introduction of hope into the caring process must be
done with sensitivity. And it may happen in many different
ways. Willingness on the part of the pastor to be relied upon
may be one way—even a willingness to take over awhile, as
with a suicidal person. It may be a declaration to persons
that even though they have given up on themselves, we will
not give up on them, because we believe that there is more
to them than just their view of themselves. The willingness
on our part to speak of our hope, and our doubt, may be
a key to showing others how to look and depend outside of
themselves. We never tell a person there is no help! Rather,
we cultivate the willingness to trust, for that is what hoping
is in many ways—the willingness to trust in promises and
move beyond defining oneself in terms of only the present
moment and experience.

In some psychological definitions of health, there is a
criterion of depending on more than recent experience for
one's source of self-esteem. In Jewish and Christian thought,
there has always been the ritual of calling on passages of
promise during times of current crisis. So, at a funeral, we
read passages like the Twenty-third Psalm or the twenty-first
chapter of Revelation with its vision of a new heaven and
a new earth where "God himself will be with them; he will
wipe away every tear from their eyes, and death shall be no
more." Those are promises that stand over against a pres-

ent-moment-oriented declaration about human nature. They call us to live out our lives on the premise that those promises are real. So is the pastoral care process to live out that belief if it is to have integrity.

THEOLOGICAL RESOURCES AND THE SANCTITY OF THE SELF

Note carefully the resources we have discussed in this chapter: repentance, including confession, guilt, and forgiveness; prayer; and hope. None of them is instantaneous. Rather, they are developmental in nature and descriptive of the processes through which we go in living out our lives. Used in the context of external power exercised by God through grace, they show respect for the limits and possibilities of human nature. Always present are the reminders of our ability and our need. Further, we are reminded that we are not wholly in charge of what we may become. Always present are assumptions that we are developing, and there seem to be cautious warnings about setting our expectations too high or too rapidly.

Sanctification is another descriptive term used in theology to discuss the attaining of likeness to God's intention for us. In the New Testament, Christians are called saints. It is not a term reserved for persons of special piety. Instead, it refers to those who have committed themselves to Christ and are consciously in the *process* of becoming more clean or pure. In the writings of Paul, sanctification is seen as an affirmation that sin is not sovereign, and the church is in a *progressive* task of gaining moral and spiritual fitness. The doctrine of justification is the affirmation that we have begun, or rather that God has started us in our process of renewal. The doctrine of sanctification is the affirmation that we are moving along!

These doctrines are theological resources to us in their

affirmation that we are special. The process of caring for one another calls for us to recognize a healthy regard for the "sanctity" of the self. These doctrines remind us of the importance of inviting rather than demanding repentance, prayer, and hope. They remind us of the dangers of attempting suddenness in change rather than process. Pastoral care is indeed a process requiring patience. Respect for the person means respect for the pace as well.

REFLECTION

In your reflection on these resources, see what others come to mind. The use of Scripture in pastoral conversations, the place of the Sacraments in pastoral care, and preaching are only a few of the other possibilities. Take some time to look at those in this chapter and others. Try to look at them in concrete ways as well as seeking to understand them conceptually.

For Further Reading

Adams, James L., and Hiltner, Seward, eds. *Pastoral Care in the Liberal Churches.* Abingdon Press, 1970.

Allport, Gordon W. *The Individual and His Religion.* Macmillan Co., 1950.

Bakus, Donald William. *The Seven Deadly Sins: Their Meaning and Measurement.* Ann Arbor, Michigan: University Microfilms, 1969.

Brister, C. W. *The Promise of Counseling.* Harper & Row, 1978.

Browning, Don S. *The Moral Context of Pastoral Care.* Westminster Press, 1976.

Brueggemann, Walter. "Covenanting as Human Vocation: A Discussion of the Relation of Bible and Pastoral Care," *Interpretation,* Vol. 33 (Spring 1979).

Colston, Lowell. *Judgment in Pastoral Counseling.* Abingdon Press, 1969.

Dicks, Russell L. *Principles and Practices of Pastoral Care.* Prentice-Hall, 1963.

Dittes, James E. *The Church in the Way.* Charles Scribner's Sons, 1967.

Faber, Heije, and Schoot, Ebel van der. *The Art of Pastoral Conversation.* Abingdon Press, 1980.

Hiltner, Seward. *Theological Dynamics.* Abingdon Press, 1972.

Hoffman, John. *Ethical Confrontation in Counseling.* University of Chicago Press, 1979.

The Interpreter's Dictionary of the Bible. 5 vols. Abingdon Press, 1962, 1976.

James, William. *The Varieties of Religious Experience.* University Books, 1963.

Klink, Thomas W. *Depth Perspectives in Pastoral Work.* Prentice-Hall, 1965.

Madden, Myron C. *The Power to Bless.* Abingdon Press, 1970.

Nouwen, Henri J. *The Wounded Healer: Ministry in Contemporary Society.* Doubleday & Co., 1972.

Oates, Wayne E. *The Psychology of Religion.* Word Books, 1973.
———. *When Religion Gets Sick.* Westminster Press, 1970.

Oglesby, Wm. B., Jr., ed. *The New Shape of Pastoral Theology: Essays in Honor of Seward Hiltner.* Abingdon Press, 1969.

Pattison, E. Mansell. *Pastor and Parish: A Systems Approach.* Fortress Press, 1977.

Pruyser, Paul W. *A Dynamic Psychology of Religion.* Harper & Row, 1968.
———. *The Minister as Diagnostician.* Westminster Press, 1976.

Sherrill, Lewis Joseph. *Guilt and Redemption.* John Knox Press, 1945.

Southard, Samuel. *Pastoral Authority in Personal Relationships.* Abingdon Press, 1969.

Strunk, Orlo, Jr., *Mature Religion.* Abingdon Press, 1965.

Tournier, Paul. *Guilt and Grace.* Harper & Row, 1962.

— PART II —
THE PERSON
OF THE PASTOR

4
Pastoral and Professional Identity: Who Am I?

"Identity" is an overworked word in our day. Because of the frequency of its usage in conversation and writing, we must be careful about how we use the term. The general meaning of the word is "sense of self." How that sense of self comes about is the interest of this chapter. We will explore the development of personal identity first. Then we will examine pastoral identity.

PERSONAL IDENTITY AND DEVELOPMENT

Significant levels of concern about identity do not emerge until adolescence. Most writers see it as a time in which the person struggles to find focus in the midst of scattered feelings. Erik Erikson refers to this era as one of "identity versus role diffusion." Ego identity is "accrued confidence that one's ability to maintain inner sameness and continuity (ego) is *matched* by the sameness and continuity of one's meaning for others." (Erik Erikson, *Identity and the Life Cycle*, p. 89.) In other words, I check out my perception of who I am with what others seem to think of me, which is no easy matter! It is difficult to be very tolerant or even pleasant if you don't know who you are and nobody else seems to know, either.

Early Development

Long before the ascendance of conscious concern, identity formation has been taking place. Erikson and others write of earlier stages that revolve around trust and mistrust, autonomy and shame, initiative and guilt, industry and inferiority. During these earlier years the storehouse for all these data has been filling steadily.

Memories and experiences have been accumulating layer upon layer, according to Erikson's epigenetic principle. We remember parents' departures and returns and whether they seemed to be glad to get back to us. We remember antics that drew a laugh and a hug, and those which got us harsh voices and angry looks. Teachers became important. We learned something about finishing tasks or having them finished by someone who seemed not to think we had ability enough to do so. Certain activities seemed "natural" and others seemed not to be "our cup of tea." All these experiences of receiving, doing, and giving gave us messages about ourselves. Then came adolescence, when we began trying to put it all together into a picture of who we were.

Adolescence

In adolescence, we become deeply conscious of positive and negative elements about ourselves. This is not to say that we didn't get euphoric or upset about ourselves in earlier years, but there is greater frequency and intensity during adolescence. Several things occur.

First, we do become deeply *conscious* of positive and negative elements about ourselves. Depending upon our previous history, we may concentrate on either the positive or the negative rather than keeping them in balance. And so we begin to experiment with those feelings and thoughts.

In my own process of moving through adolescence, there was a deep sense that I was "supposed" to be a doctor. That held until I found out more about what doctors do. College chemistry, in particular, convinced me that I had misunderstood my calling. So if helping people was what I was meant to do, the next option seemed to be psychology. Diagnostic testing and running rats through mazes also left something to be desired. My experiment had ruled out one more option. Then came ministry, which for me was the kind of helping that seemed to fit. The process is one of coming to terms with positive and negative elements in one's sense of self. Experiments are going on all the time, some conscious and many unconscious, to narrow down the choices. The same sorts of experiments are going on with relationships to parents, friends, and potential lifetime partners. Tentative emotional commitments are made to the one we were meant to spend our life with. Then we find some things we didn't know about that person. And the search goes on! The process varies in intensity and longevity, but the consciousness is there and remains there for many years.

Mobility, specializations, multiple numbers of people and cultures confront us with a longer choosing process. In fact, the process is so complex that we see many casualties from it—people who live out their lives never being able to "make up their mind." As the front page of one magazine portrayed it, a man looks wistfully out into the face of the reader and says, "I'm fifty years old, and I still haven't decided what I want to be when I grow up."

In addition to new consciousness in adolescence, we become *capable* of perceiving and abiding by values of our own choosing. Capability revolves around the issue of dependence. Until this stage in life we have been relatively content to rely on others to make choices for us and to define the limits within which we live. The new consciousness of ourselves now brings the ability and desire to check out the system within which we have lived. We begin to experiment with our values.

During the elementary school years, science projects and other experiments take place that center on what the child can *do*. With adolescence, experiments revolve around what I can and will *believe*. Unfortunately, many people fail to recognize these times as experimental and respond as if they were final decisions. So, the teenager who wants to attend another church is seen as "deserting the faith." The adolescent who says, "So what's wrong with sex on a first date?" elicits an intense response from the parent. And, of course, when we respond with such intensity, we have set the stage for further experiments. "Gee, if they get that upset about that one, I wonder what will happen if I . . ."

In brief, the adolescent is capable of committing himself or herself to some value system. Passion has emerged, and there are many causes and people lying around to get passionate about.

A third element in adolescence revolves around the issue of *fidelity*. I am now capable of being faithful to some ideological view and to particular people by choice! In the church, we have usually talked about this in terms of vocation.

Identity and Vocation

Vocation is, of course, a good theological word. It comes from the sense of "being called." Our calling is, in theological terms, to seek out and live out God's intentions for us. The adolescent struggles to discover and live out who he or she is "meant to be," whether viewed as a religious quest or not.

Historically and popularly, calling and vocation have been tied too closely to religious "jobs." They have not been properly understood in the deeper meaning of a "style of life." Much of the work of the Reformation was centered on trying to correct that popular understanding. Luther, in particular, sought to show that the roles of spouse, parent, child, employer, employee, etc., are all expressions of a more central sense of vocation. Calvin, more activist in his reflection than Luther, saw calling and vocation to include a sense of social responsibility. One is called to demonstrate actively the marks of one's "elect" position and vocation.

In summary, vocation carries a sense of purpose for one's life that is not self-created. Purposeful living involves a search for one's sense of vocation, described in psychological terms as the search for identity. Most of us can report a time, even if not lasting, in which we were searching for what it was that we were supposed to be. External factors are sought in the decision and discovery, as well as internal ones. Calvin, in writing about one's calling to ministry, speaks of the importance of both an inner and an outer call to be confirmed in the choice of ordained ministry as one's vocation. The principle could be generalized usefully to include *any* sense of vocation.

The Need for a System

Consciousness, capability, and faithfulness propel people to find the system within which they can comfortably and responsibly live out their identity, their sense of self. If I do not have such a system to which I subscribe, then I experience what Erikson calls role diffusion. There is no source of appeal in making my decisions about how I live. A sense of self, identity, provides stability. It is a commitment to more than myself. It is a commitment to a system within which I fit.

Several implications come from the importance of gaining a sense of personal identity. First, if I am not faithful to a system that is consonant with my sense of identity, I remain at the mercy of the multiple requests that bombard me from all sides. They often are more than requests. They are temptations and pressures from institutions as well as individuals. As children we could always appeal to the system that "my parents won't let me" or "because my parents said so" to screen out demands. As adults we need another authority that goes beyond parental expectations. If I do not have some system or authority, then I remain at the mercy of more emotional needs such as the need to have everyone like me, the need to obey anyone who sounds authoritative, the need to work hard because "everybody else" does, the need to avoid discomfort. Those needs become the authority in my life. Adolescence is the stage in which we have the opportunity to establish a system, or new authority, in a still somewhat protected context.

A second implication of the importance of a system may be drawn from the numbers of people who remain in the stage of searching which we call adolescence. The culture provides many places for the unprepared to live in relative protection for short or long periods of time if unable to make commitments. Military service and graduate schools are a couple of examples. Many in those places are developing the identity to which they have committed themselves. There also are many who find those places a good protected spot where decisions will be made for them.

A third implication is that identity cannot be pursued in isolation. The concept of system presupposes a framework consisting of more than one person. Identity is worked out in *relationship*. It is a choice of role, and role exists in relationship to another or others. Identity involves the accrual of a sense of sameness and continuity that is matched by a relatively similar perception of oneself by others.

PASTORAL IDENTITY AND COMMITMENT

Professional identity is a subsystem of personal identity. It should be an outgrowth of and consonant with the choice or commitment to a particular system or ideology. Professional identity would not be possible if a person had not acquired an awareness of personal history and styles of response, the sense of self. Faithfulness to a system of belief is important. Such a commitment clearly defines the professional identity by distinguishing what can be offered to another person and the form in which it is offered.

Pastoral Identity and Personal History

Pastoral identity involves a particular expression of the sense of self. It is more than doing a job. It is a "living out" of the sense of self.

Awareness of personal history plays an important part in this, much of it revolving around our hopes and points of dread. For example, the death of my mother by cancer is a point of focus for me in my ministry. There is the hope that I can minister to persons with cancer with the compassion I wanted for my mother. There is a level of dread whenever I visit someone with cancer, because it brings back memories of my mother's death. That experience, both in the hopes and the dread it brings to me now, provides some professional or pastoral focus for the living out of my identity. Experiences as a child at summer church camp provide awareness and focus for my ministry. I want to provide such experiences for others because they were good for me, and I believe myself able to provide that for others. At the same time, there is some dread in me about leading a church camp for young people, because I remember some of the things that they may be pulling off behind my back, just as I did to counselors myself!

Pastoral Identity and Faithfulness to a System

More than awareness of personal history is necessary to function in a pastoral identity. There must also be commitment to a system of belief, an ideology, a theology. The *pastoral* function is really a role definition. There is a long tradition of what it means to be a pastor. Much of the literature refers to it as the *shepherding* function. Involved are particular concerns for people and particular styles of relating to them. In the New Testament, for instance, the shepherding or pastoral task is a form of teaching (Eph. 4:11; John 21:15–17). A way of relating to or caring for people is taught to others in both word and action.

Historically, the four functions of pastoral care have been healing, guiding, sustaining, and reconciling. Each of them has as its aim the "maintenance" or strengthening of people to live with their humanness in more effective ways, or with integrity. Being pastoral, then, involves modeling for persons a way of living, identifying resources for them or reminding them of resources that they may have forgotten.

Much good literature about styles of pastoral care is available to us in biblical, theological, and historical writing. One of our modern definitions of being a professional includes the element of "mastery of a body of knowledge." That body of knowledge is necessary for a pastor if she or he is to function professionally and pastorally in a real sense. It is not just a personal experience, but the identification with a whole history of experience.

Pastoral Identity and Identification

As pastor, a man or woman expects and is expected to "identify" with other people. It is assumed that you wish to "be with" people during significant and routine moments in their lives. Personal expectation *and* historical expectation play a part in that statement. The language of ordination in many traditions is "set apart," but the intention of that "set apart-ness" is to free us to be with people in their growth. A pastor takes responsibility for a congregation and agrees to be with them, to serve "among" them.

Reflecting Old and New Testament themes, the pastor is representative of the reality of God's living among us. In the Christian faith, Jesus is understood as the fulfillment of

God's being with us. He identifies with us. That is the reality of the incarnation. The role of the pastor is to live out the function of being among the people, a representative of God's grace among us.

So, the role of the pastor is to identify with the very people to whom we minister. In that sense, the pastor does not distance himself or herself from people according to the dictates of some other helping professions. Distance is not necessarily a bad thing as a helping act, and there may be times when the pastor must or should use it. But it is only in the context of presence that exercises of absence or distance take on special meaning.

Part of identifying with people means affirming that we are like them. We too are sinners. That provides us all with a sense of commonality and mutuality. And it is in that context that trust can develop.

Pastoral Identity and Authority

As representative, the pastor also claims the authority of a system as well as of self. We move about in our role as pastor not only because we want to (and some days we don't even want to!) but also because we are instructed to do so by the system to which we have committed ourselves. The system is both political and theological. Church polity describes our duties as pastors, and theology clarifies the authority under which we operate. That theology and polity also describe limits for us. Requests will be made of us that we may want to perform out of concern for or identification with a person, but polity prevents us from doing so. The authority is not simply our own. It is from the system, the tradition of which we are a part.

In our development as pastors it is important that we continue to grow in our willingness to *acknowledge* the authority under which we live and to *claim* the authority which we carry by virtue of being pastor. Certainly we also build up a history with people that gives us authority by virtue of our loyalty and faithfulness to them over a period of time. That too is a part of our understanding of identity. But our authority is more than that. We are representatives of God! Heavy as the phrase may sound, it is so by virtue of our commitment to the system.

This authority expresses itself in several ways. One of them involves the manner in which we handle questions and requests that come to us. Our authority presses us to look more closely. The pastoral response might be to change the question instead of answering it, to press the person to look more closely. Acts 3 illustrates the point in Peter's and John's response to the lame man asking for silver and gold. Instead, they ask if he would like to be healed and walk again. Such responses can be made to persons in need of seeing the vision of growth more clearly. Our commitment to an authority, a system, frees us to respond to people at deeper levels rather than being caught in having to please them. By changing the question we may enlarge the quest for the person rather than fulfilling the more immediate expectation.

Interestingly enough, in research carried out with encounter group leaders in the early 1970s leaders who had a commitment to a particular theoretical system seemed to have greater success with group members than those who attempted to remain "value free." (Morton A. Lieberman, Irvin D. Yalom, and Matthew B. Miles, *Encounter Groups: First Facts,* p. 435.) Part of the security of a system is having a way to understand what is happening. It provides a frame of reference. Without such a system, which in our case is our theological understanding, the pastor is left at the mercy of the request and the more personal needs to gain approval (or in some cases, rejection).

Many seminary students and pastors become intensely uncomfortable or irritated at being called "preacher" or

"Reverend." For some there is resentment at being put in a role that may limit their pursuit of personal interests and enjoyments. They are right. The professional identity, by definition, contains certain expectations. The discomfort may be a clue to the seriousness of the commitment. A student should examine such resentment closely to see whether it is a signal calling for growth and renewed commitment or a signal that this is not the identity that fits. Others are more fearful than irritated at the title. They sense the pressure of expectation and are anxious about their ability or character to carry out the tasks. Growth, for them, consists of gaining familiarity and comfort with that system.

In a massive survey carried out by the Readiness for Ministry Project of the Association of Theological Schools, much study focused on lay expectations of ministers. (David S. Schuller, Merton P. Strommen, and Milo L. Brekke, *Ministry in America.*) Skill was of less importance than integrity, evidence of real commitment to the faith. That demonstrates an authority that goes beyond the person. And it is an authority to which people will respond.

Pastoral Identity and Being a Person

It is important to realize that pastoral identity is not the living of a religious life. In fact, the pastoral identity often interferes with it. Pastoral identity is a narrowing of scope. It is a role definition, a specialization that should be *an* expression of personal identity, but should not be viewed as *the* expression of personal identity. A large part of the role is giving, and that is not enough for a fulfilling personal sense of self. Both the experience of living out a personal identity and the exercise of one's faithfulness to a religious system must be more broad than the exercise of a particular role.

Specialization, the exercise of a professional identity, may interfere at times with personal identity. Plans to enjoy a party are interfered with by people who, upon seeing the minister, decide to ask for help or advice. Their courage is up then, more so than when they debated whether to call at the church. Speech, behavior, and community involvement are affected by the perception that you are *the minister.*

On the other hand, personal identity often aids the expression of pastoral identity. You have chosen that particular role because of particular personal gifts and abilities you have, ones that are appreciated by others. Other interests, not ordinarily connected with the professional role, may contribute to greater expertise. I was quite struck with a professor of Bible who once said that his interest in bird-watching had been a real asset to him in exegesis. Asked to explain, he pointed out that bird-watching requires great patience, long waiting, persistent watching and listening for minute sounds, flight patterns, etc. The result could be the identification of a species or behavior pattern not seen before. In like manner, his exegetical method had come to appreciate the value of waiting, watching, remaining open to an innuendo, a variation that might yield new understanding of the text.

Pastors and theological students often complain of the lack of apparent concern with prayer life, experience of community, authentic study of Scripture, etc., on the campus of a theological seminary. The atmosphere is too abstract, cold, and "scholarly," they say. While the issue deserves attention, remember also that the task of a theological seminary is to provide the skills necessary to carry out the *role* of ministry. Many of the complaints revolve around the absence of resources for the fulfillment of the *person.* At that point the *persons* involved have the awareness and the capability of designing and carrying out programs that are helpful in their overall development.

The problem remains the same in the exercise of parish

ministry and the specialized ministries. Too often we look to the professional life as the resource to the personal, when the reverse should be the case.

Pressure on the pastoral role to yield benefits that enrich our entire personal identity usually results in a distorted professional life and a deprived personal one. We can court people to need us and then resent the imposition on our personal time. The pattern becomes entrenched, resulting in bitterness in all spheres of our living. Knowledge of these dynamics of identity are important to us as we design an aware and realistic rhythm of living—one that makes us effective in our pastoral role and at the same time leaves us protected and free to enjoy our personal identity in its broader dimensions.

REFLECTION

Before we move into the next chapter to discuss some of the particular elements associated with the pastoral role of the minister, some personal reflection is in order. Think of an event in which a pastor is likely to be involved. Perhaps it is a funeral, a wedding, a worship service, or a hospital visit. Write down the things *you* think are expected of the pastor in that situation. List formal duties as well as personal hopes about the manner in which those duties are carried out. Get as many of your public and private expectations down on paper as possible.

Having done that, talk to several other persons about the event you have chosen and ask them about their expectations. Compare their lists with your own. Are they similar or different? What kinds of things do you think have come to play in your formulation of your list and the formulations of people other than yourself? Try to identify those which are based on personal need and those which come from tradition. How often are they identical or similar?

It is helpful to survey the expectations of many people. Take those differing perspectives seriously. Think about guidelines that are useful in distinguishing appropriate and inappropriate expectations. It is helpful to us in watching out for overly narrowed goals for ourselves.

Equally important with surveys is familiarity with history. Read some of the books listed at the end of this chapter, or at least skim parts of some of them. Read your own polity with an eye for the perceptions of the pastoral role. Keep yourself in conversation with all of them. It is important for your own pastoral development that you are aware of them, even if not always in agreement with them.

For Further Reading

Baxter, Richard. *The Reformed Pastor.* Ed. John T. Wilkinson. London: Epworth Press, 1939.

Capps, Donald. *Pastoral Care: A Thematic Approach.* Westminster Press, 1979.

Clebsch, William A., and Jaekle, Charles R. *Pastoral Care in Historical Perspective.* Prentice-Hall, 1964.

Dittes, James E. *When the People Say No: Conflict and the Call to Ministry.* Harper & Row, 1979.

Erikson, Erik H. *Identity and the Life Cycle.* International Universities Press, 1959.

————. *Identity: Youth and Crisis.* W. W. Norton & Co., 1968.

Hiltner, Seward. *The Christian Shepherd.* Abingdon Press, 1959.

————. *Ferment in the Ministry.* Abingdon Press, 1969.

Lieberman, Morton A.; Yalom, Irvin D.; and Miles, Matthew B. *Encounter Groups: First Facts.* Basic Books, 1973.

Oates, Wayne E. *The Christian Pastor,* Revised and Enlarged. Westminster Press, 1980.

————. *On Becoming Children of God.* Westminster Press, 1969.

Schuller, David S.; Strommen, Merton P.; and Brekke, Milo L. *Ministry in America.* Harper & Row, 1980.
Wise, Carroll A. *The Meaning of Pastoral Care.* Harper & Row, 1966.

5

Functions
of the Pastor

With some understanding of pastoral identity, our focus now turns to pastoral *functions*. What we *do* as pastors must be shaped by the theology or system to which we have committed ourselves. One of the most helpful exercises during my own graduate study was in this vein. My requirement was to read John Calvin's *Institutes of the Christian Religion* and extrapolate a theology of pastoral care. Groan though I did, it is an exercise I consider to be important for any persons seeking to take theology seriously in their practice of pastoral care. Certainly John Calvin is not the one to whom everyone should turn. A reputable theologian from your own tradition should be chosen.

My own conclusion at that time was that pastoral care should direct itself to five aims: (1) to make human beings aware of their true condition (awareness of sin, limits, gifts, etc.); (2) to make human beings aware of God as Creator and Redeemer (awareness of the freedom that is available in the midst of our existence); (3) to relate persons to one another (importance of the community in our living); (4) to guide persons in their response to the grace of God in their lives (to view the caring process as more than crisis-oriented); and (5) to bring theology to bear on the life experiences of people (the discipline of the believer). Aims derived in such a way aid us in arriving at concrete functions and the way in which we carry them out.

Pastoral care involves a belief that an understanding of who we are is an essential task. We must seek to understand ourselves in our strengths and weaknesses, as well as in our relationships with each other and with God, if we are to live out our vocation effectively. Bringing about such understanding and living is the aim of pastoral care. That aim manifests itself in at least three major functions: representative, servant, and carrier of tradition.

THE PASTOR AS REPRESENTATIVE

Earlier references have been made to the representative function of the pastor. Authority for the pastor is derived from it. Any claim to self-importance, any claim to special knowledge, is secondary to the authority that is claimed as a representative of God. Personal claims convey that the minister is, in some way, better than the person to whom she or he ministers. The claim to be a representative affirms that the minister *identifies* with the person to whom he or she ministers. Commonality and necessity are affirmed.

Calvin expresses the matter helpfully in answering the question of why people should be needed or used to serve as pastors. He points out that God

> could indeed do it either by himself without any sort of aid or instrument, or even by the angels; but there are many reasons why he prefers to do it by means of men. . . . This is the best and most useful exercise in humility, when he accustoms us to obey his Word, even though it be preached through men like us and sometimes even by those of lower worth than we. . . . When a puny man risen from the dust speaks in God's name, at this point we best evidence our piety

and obedience toward God if we show ourselves
teachable toward his minister, although he excels us
in nothing. (Calvin: *Institutes of the Christian Religion*,
ed. by John T. McNeill, The Library of Christian
Classics, IV. iii. 1, pp. 1053–1054; Westminster
Press, 1967)

Representative authority, then, is a fascinating blend of
power and humility. We can, on the one hand, speak with
conviction, and on the other hand, claim a commonality
with those to whom we speak.

Not only do we claim to represent God when going as
minister to another person. By derivation we are also representatives of the human community, the church. The bonds
of commonality and necessity that characterize that community are very applicable here. Initiative is exercised on behalf of the human community as well as on behalf of God.
The invitation is more than that of a person who happens
to be a minister. The faithfulness that is exhibited is more
than that of one person. They are initiative and faithfulness
from God *and* his people.

The invitation we offer as representative is usually limited
or distorted at the same time as it is warm and caring. As
Calvin reminded us, it is offered through "a puny [person]
risen from the dust." Similarities between the one offering
and the one receiving the invitation, then, are obvious.
What will happen in any particular event of caring is never
known by pastor or parishioner. So, the invitation is shaky
at times. We feel awkward. But the invitation also carries
with it the knowledge that it may be the word of the Lord.
Speaking of the word of the Lord makes the task shaky,
anxiety-producing. It seems audacious to presume to carry
the word of the Lord to someone. And we will often find
out that it wasn't! But there is also the possibility that it is
. . . and we may never know.

One of the struggles of ministry is with the concept of authority. To whom am *I* to go? What authority can I claim? What right do I have to presume? The answers are not always clear, but the confessional standards that formed the basis for this approach to initiative seem to say that it is there. It is not our personal authority, because that indeed would be presumptuous. It is not the authority to mandate another person's decisions and actions. Rather, it is a limited authority—the authority to go on behalf of a community and our God, to say that we have noticed. And we go to say that what we have seen and whom we have seen matter to us.

So, we go as representatives. We go wherever we see something happening that calls for initiative and faithfulness. That's not all there is to it, of course. There is a form that is called for. And it will be discussed in the next section. But our representative function authorizes us to go. Our own finitude calls for us to set some limits on what we expect of ourselves, as well as what we expect of those to whom we go. Otherwise, we will move beyond responsible representation to compulsive action, blind to our needs and limits, in need of someone taking initiative toward us! And we may miss some of the gifts we have to offer as well.

As representatives we go both burdened with and relieved of responsibility. The responsibility is to go and extend an invitation on behalf of ourselves, our community of faith, and God. We are relieved of the responsibility of being dependent on the results of those meetings as the final evaluative criteria for our own work.

The resources of pastoral care which were discussed in Chapter 3 become appropriate and authorized by our representative function. Repentance, forgiveness, prayer, and hope all presume a higher authority in order to carry meaning. We could not offer those resources with *personal* promises about their value. Only in our *representative* function do those promises become real.

Only in our functioning as representative can we speak with authority in our preaching, in our teaching, and in our exercise of pastoral care. The process of moral inquiry to which Don Browning points us in *The Moral Context of Pastoral Care,* for instance, claims the minister's role as representative. People look to us for an "authoritative" word on the ways in which they should grapple with the difficult and pleasurable moments in their life's journey. Care must be exercised on our part so that we both claim that authority and at the same time not abuse it in a manipulative ploy to make sure that the person not dare to differ with us. Such manipulation would desecrate the authority which we claim.

THE PASTOR AS SERVANT

Misuse and abuse of power evidence themselves around us daily. Five minutes of leafing through the day's newspaper yields many examples. Such distortion of power is no less likely in the exercise of the authority of a minister. Our discussions of human nature remind us of the liabilities that are present as well as the possibilities.

No doubt the choice of "servant" as a descriptive term for the minister alerts us to the temptations that authority brings. The principles and resources we have reviewed reinforce the concept of the function of servant. Initiative as a principle means that I go to others rather than demanding that they come to me. Faithfulness, our second principle, connotes that we do something *for* others rather than requiring that they do something for us. A representative who functions as servant directs himself or herself toward others rather than expecting them to direct themselves toward us.

Furthermore, the resources of repentance, forgiveness, prayer, and hope are disciplines that point to a higher authority. They are expected of us as well as of those whom we serve. They are resources in which we participate for the benefit of those we serve rather than rituals required of others for our own aggrandizement.

Servant: one whose authority lies elsewhere. That is who we are. See the illustrations of it throughout Scripture. Moses is called by God to lead a great people, Israel, out of Egypt. Following instructions drew him commendations. Assuming and asserting authority of his own kept him with only a vision of the Promised Land.

Job is the man to whom we often refer as faithful servant and model of patience. That was not the case, however. On many occasions he was bitter and questioning about his apparent punishment without just cause. The final note of that Old Testament book is a message to Job: "Who are you to question?" He is reminded that he is servant.

The New Testament gives us perspective on the role of servant as well. Jesus defines himself as servant. The Gospel of Mark provides examples of commendation for service and chastisement for attempts to assert authority that is out of line with Jesus' instructions. (Cf. James L. Mays, ". . . And She Served Them," *As I See It,* Vol. IX, No. 2, Nov. 1978.)

Servants. That is who we are. Look at the more typical understanding of the pastoral role. Listening is a role into which we are placed time and time again. It is important that we hear and seek to understand the person who wants to be heard. Often we experience frustration at not being able to do more than that. Some other helping disciplines, unable to find solutions, would recommend that we move on to the people we can help. But pastoral care places a premium on the importance of faithfulness over results. And so we stay, serving by listening and remaining.

Another understanding of the pastoral function as servant involves the role of teaching. One service we provide is that of reminding. In the times we sit and listen and hear the question, "What am I to do?" We may remind people of resources not in mind at the moment. Our willingness to speak, sometimes forcefully, is a service often not provided by others. Our belief that there is something to be learned in life experiences may offer new vision to another person.

Defining oneself as here to serve should occur with regularity in ministry. When a pastor enters a hospital room, knocks on a front door, greets a person at the church office, or meets parishioners and friends on the street, the function of pastor as servant should evidence itself. "Hi, I'm Bill Arnold, the minister of —————— Church. I wanted to come by, see how you're doing, and find out if there are ways I could be helpful." "Do you really mean you're that tired? Let's find out if something can be done to deal with that." "John, I haven't seen you in a good while, and wanted to find out what has been going on in your world." Such inquiries about another person's welfare can and should be made in a manner that offers interest and availability without seeming to count on the person's having serious problems.

A trusted servant is often confided in. A pompous authority is seldom trusted with confidences. The servant, interestingly enough, has a power that in some ways is powerless. Because the power does not enable the servant representative to do anything *to* the other person, it is a power that *enables* that other person to reveal and struggle with issues heretofore avoided.

In the mix of representative authority and servanthood, we possess the ability to choose the resources to be offered to those for whom we care. We have spoken earlier of the importance of commitment to a system of belief in one's pastoral identity. Such commitment frees the pastor from slavery to whatever request is made of her or him. So, when the pastor-servant inquires or is approached by persons in need, there is not an enslavement to do or provide whatever is requested. Instead, our principles and resources are applied with care and discretion. To the person who asks that we pray for him or her to die, we may so pray, *or* we may refuse. Our refusal may take the form of offering to pray that God will let the person know that his or her suffering is known to him, and that the burdens will be relieved. *Then,* instead of leaving after the prayer as expected, we may stay to listen to the pain through which that person is passing. Faithful servant, yes. Slave to the request? No.

One of my favorite questions for many years when I was doing a screening interview with a person interested in clinical pastoral education was built around a personal experience. An amputee, after requesting that I as chaplain come to his room, asked me to pray for his leg to grow back. My refusal to do so, accompanied by a willingness to hear his grief about the loss, resulted in a good learning experience for me. Had I prayed too quickly, according to his wishes, not only would I have violated my own understanding of prayer, but I would not have met his deeper need to come to terms with his loss. Asking students what they would do in such a case has been a quick way to get to the tension of being authority and servant at the same time.

THE PASTOR AS CARRIER OF TRADITION

The search for some sort of stability brings many people to the pastor's doorstep. They know what to expect, they think, when they come. Certainly there are other helping professions around, some of which may be more helpful. But people don't always know what that other professional may be up to. There is a tradition that has been around a long time about what ministers are up to, and whether the stereotypes are right or not, people come because they have clear expectations.

Tradition carries a great deal of power in people's minds.

Ministry has a long tradition. That is part of its authority—longevity. "If it lasts, it must be worth something." That is the rationale that brings many persons. A minister is expected to be dependable and consistent. That is what ministers have "always" been.

In fact, ministers in the pastoral role, as well as others, do have a tradition about what is offered when they come to parishioner or parishioner comes to them. Characteristically, those pastoral functions have been fourfold, with varying emphases in different historical periods.

The first of those four has been *healing*. At one time, when sickness of body or mind struck, the minister was the only one called. The healing process was in his or her hands. Soundness of body, mind, and spirit has historically been the concern of the minister. And in our day of greater specialization with psychology and medicine, the minister is still called frequently when sickness occurs. That particular presence of one who represents God and the community of faith brings comfort and often healing, both symbolically and concretely.

The second traditional role has been that of *sustaining*. When health of some kind is not restored, the task remains of working out how to live with the situation. That is the time when many of the specialties, by their tradition, withdraw. Ministry, however, goes on. The minister may be the one to help bring in other specialties of sustenance, such as visiting nurses, social workers, community agencies, long-term therapists. Continuity is provided by a pastor who goes through both crisis and aftermath, reinforcing the principles of initiative and faithfulness. Continuing to visit in the nursing home as well as in the hospital and continuing to see the family after a death when others have returned to life as normal, provide sustenance. The minister is freed to offer sustained interest in such people by the community of faith. He or she comes in their name and in God's name, and gratitude should be expressed to God and that community for enabling the minister to come.

Counseling, advising, or disciplining constitute a third historical function of the pastor. Healing and sustaining traditions equip the minister to remain with people in various ways. The need also exists for telling or teaching them something. These functions are more forceful movements in the service of others.

A twenty-one-year-old married woman was referred to her pastor for counseling. She was experiencing a variety of conflicts in her marriage, with her children, and on her job. She came to the first meeting demanding that the minister do something "right now" because she "couldn't stand it another minute." After the pastor listened for an hour and attempted to provide some sustaining interest, the following dialogue took place:

> PASTOR: Mrs. _____, I would like to set up an appointment with you for next week.
> PARISHIONER: I don't want another appointment! You've got to do something right this minute. If you don't do something today, I'm not coming back.
> PASTOR: You sound so overwhelmed with all this, I wish we could solve it all quickly, but we can't. Let's make our plans for next week and continue to work on it.
> PARISHIONER: Don't you hear me? (She cries hysterically.) I want help now!
> PASTOR: Mrs. _____, you have about four alternatives, as I see it. You can run away from your husband, your family, your job, and try to start all over by yourself; you can hospitalize yourself; you can just continue to live in the mess you are in; or you can commit yourself to seeing me or another counselor on a regular basis with the hope that we can help you to work things out. I think we can help. But the thing

that needs to be done right now is for you to see that
you have to make a choice, and there's nothing I can
do until you commit yourself to some choice.

Whether or not we would agree with the particular style of
that pastor, his situation illustrates the need for times of
firmness and direction.

Less dramatic examples of counsel and advice might have
been given. Many times the process takes the form of
friendly conversation. Suggestions can be made without the
demand that they be accepted. The aim is to provide resources that might not have been seen otherwise. The counseling, advising role constitutes a teaching frame of reference in pastoral care. We speak as well as listen, and at
carefully chosen times.

The fourth traditional expression of pastoral care is *reconciling.* In marriage counseling, family counseling, group
meetings, and work, there are always relationship difficulties. Ministering to relationships is the focus of reconciliation, reflecting the theological affirmation that we were
created to live more fully in relationships of many kinds.
Commonality and necessity raise their heads again.
Through listening, suggesting, teaching, and just showing
interest, we minister to relationships. We provide a relationship that has health, we hope. Through *using us* (servanthood), people may gain help in returning to relationships
with new understanding and determination to enrich them.
If those relationships do not survive, we continue to minister to people in their grief and disappointment. They need
relationships then, just as in other moments, and all too
often people cut them off, or they cut themselves off.

By tradition, we as ministers will be called when there is
sickness, when there is hopelessness, when advice is needed,
and when relationships are in pain. This is so because it has
been so for centuries. That tradition will be expected of us.

It gives us authority, and it defines us as here to serve, to be used in difficult times. The knowledge that we are around gives a sense of stability to many persons. It is a crucial function in our living out the identity of pastor.

REFLECTION

As you conclude the reading of this chapter and this part on identity, take some time to reflect on how these functions of ministry fit with your sense of call. Imagine your response to a late-night call to the bedside of a dying person. Give thought to your expectations of yourself when a young person calls to discuss whether to go to college or get a job. What happens when you get the news that a couple in your congregation have separated, and one of them is involved in an affair with still another member of the congregation? Those are some of the situations you will face as pastor. These are the functions generally prescribed as the domain of the minister.

Such matters call for careful reflection on what ministry is and how you will exercise it in a way that fits with your understanding of yourself. Those issues also call for help beyond your training and self-understanding, and that is the reason for our next part on the disciplines of support.

For Further Reading

Bennett, George. *When They Ask for Bread.* John Knox Press, 1978.

Browning, Don S. *The Moral Context of Pastoral Care.* Westminster Press, 1976.

Clebsch, William A., and Jaekle, Charles R. *Pastoral Care in Historical Perspective.* Prentice-Hall, 1964.

Clinebell, Howard J., Jr. *Basic Types of Pastoral Counseling.* Abingdon Press, 1966.

Dittes, James E. *The Church in the Way.* Charles Scribner's Sons, 1967.

Hiltner, Seward. *The Christian Shepherd.* Abingdon Press, 1959.

McNeill, John T. *A History of the Cure of Souls.* Harper & Row, 1977.

Nouwen, Henri J. *The Living Reminder.* Seabury Press, 1977.

———. *The Wounded Healer.* Doubleday & Co., 1972.

Oates, Wayne E. *The Christian Pastor,* Revised and Enlarged. Westminster Press, 1980.

———, ed. Christian Care Books. A series of 12 practical guides for help in dealing with difficult problems. Westminster Press, 1980.

Pruyser, Paul W. *The Minister as Diagnostician.* Westminster Press, 1976.

Schuller, David S.; Strommen, Merton P.; and Brekke, Milo L. *Ministry in America.* Harper & Row, 1980.

— PART III —
THE DISCIPLINES
OF SUPPORT

6
Comparative Views
of Human Nature

Many varieties of helping professions exist; many theories and methodologies influence them. All are based on views of human nature, some explicit and others unarticulated. Just as we continue to study our theology for deeper understanding, so we must examine the views of human nature within the other supporting disciplines. Often they will provide us with new insights into our theological understanding. Often they will prove so out of accord with our ground of understanding that we will have to proceed very cautiously in our use of them.

There are at least five important frames of reference for reflection and discussion. They will be used to compare the theological assumptions forwarded earlier in this book and assumptions drawn from the human potential movement.

BELIEFS ABOUT GROWTH

Built around interpretations of writers such as Gordon Allport and Abraham Maslow, many approaches in the human potential movement provide varying levels of encouragement to the effect that "you can become who you want to be." That process of becoming is engineered in various ways. There may be intense interpersonal work or heavy indoctrination in a theoretical system. Whatever the system used, the common belief being conveyed is that "you can change." Approaches such as transactional analysis, encounter group methodology, and Gestalt therapy are rich in suggestions for leaders to use in bringing about, or enabling, change in the patients or clients with whom they work.

The first theological question of these approaches regards the changeability of human beings. How necessary is such change? How changeable are we? The discussion must revolve around the concepts of optimism and sin.

These pop psychologies do have a word of encouragement to offer us about change, but they also promise more than they can deliver from this author's theological perspective. Psychologies of change do not always acknowledge limits very effectively, engendering instead a sense of "I must not have done it right" when one fails to achieve the change hoped for. All too often persons return from encounter groups, marathon weekends, and some forms of therapy in a state of high elation. Those same persons later experience depression when they discover that the change didn't last. The danger of an overly optimistic emphasis on change and growth is the accompanying failure to learn to live with limits, to forget that we are not God.

Second, unmoderated optimism places a merciless burden on the self. If one believes that dramatic changes *can* be brought about, then there is an obligation to do so or else be considered incompetent or a failure. When a change is attempted that has been *promised* as possible, the resultant feeling when it doesn't work is that I view myself *as* a failure instead of having *experienced* a failure. The difference is subtle but important. If I *am* a failure, my being has become identified with my experience. My worth is entirely dependent on what I do. The definition of self is changed from a question of who I am created to be to a dependency on what I do as the ultimate determinant of my worth and sense of being. Works righteousness is always lurking in the background.

Obviously, the beliefs we hold about limitations and sin must be placed in conversation with optimism about human potential. We risk the danger of overemphasizing limits and sin. Too much such emphasis can strip a person of motivation for *any* change! What has been so attractive to people about the human potential movement is the assurance that they *can* do something about difficult experiences. Human potential techniques may be highly useful *if* they are used to convey that individuals have the *freedom* to pursue change without denying their limitations and without the outcome of the attempted changes being a judgment on their sense of worth.

In consulting with or making a referral to another supporting discipline, we must watch for the kinds of promises that are made to us and to the person on whose behalf we are working. The optimism and affirmation of human limits that are conveyed will make a great difference in the kind of care that is rendered.

THE VALUE PLACED ON FEELINGS

Emotions, or feelings, are viewed quite differently among helping professionals. Those who consider themselves cognitive in their approach avoid calling for much emotional exposure from a client, controlling the helping process in a manner that explores the person's beliefs and value assumptions. Many who are involved in the human potential movement, on the other hand, place heavy emphasis on the importance of the emotions. Feelings, they maintain, are dependable indicators of the person's true orientation. All too often, the feelings have been blocked, resulting in a life that is blocked from growing to its true potential. "Getting the feelings out" is an essential ingredient in the therapeutic process. Encounter groups and Gestalt therapy, in particular, have acquired a reputation for intensity of feeling as a major component of their helping process.

Certainly the emotions are taken seriously in our theological traditions, and there is variety within them about the level of expression that is encouraged. Some groups are warm and expressive of their faith, while others remain cool, intellectual, and restrained. In Presbyterian circles the joke recurs that John Calvin misunderstood biblical references to "God's chosen people" and created a denomination that seemed to be "God's frozen people" in terms of expressed emotion.

Idolatry of one dimension of existence over others is the danger to be watched for theologically. Certainly, emotion is a part of our faith. But so also is rational thought. We are a people of *belief,* and those beliefs are often used to evaluate the integrity of feelings. Feelings may be authentic expressions of love or righteous indignation. At the same time they may be expressions of our distortions in perspective, so that our loving or anger may be manipulative and controlling, rather than genuine.

When consulting with or making a referral to another helping professional, find out about his or her approach in terms of dealing with feelings. They are a vital part of our human experience, but they should not be dealt with to the exclusion of the other expressions of our humanness.

PERSPECTIVE ON TIME

Much of the human potential movement places heavy emphasis on the "present moment." It is an emphasis on the "here and now," and discussions of personal history, the "there and then," are viewed frequently as attempts to resist the therapeutic process. Other approaches, such as traditional psychoanalysis, spend a vast amount of time on personal history and enabling persons to understand how their past experiences have led them to become who they are now. Other therapists, utilizing a form of optimism, will focus on the future. "Don't worry about what you have been or what you are now," they say. "Just remember that you can become whatever you want to be if you will believe in yourself."

There would be no argument about the importance of any of these perspectives on time from a theological perspective. The dispute would occur over the propriety of choosing one of them over against the other two. An adequate and holistic view of human nature will not lower the importance of one or two of these perspectives in deference to the other and remain faithful to the understanding of who we are.

We are, theologically, creatures with a crucial history. God's promises tell us who we are and who we are created to be. Those promises and instructions enable us to live in the present moment, recognizing that our decisions are important and make a difference. And those promises, given in the past and shaping us in so many ways, also point to the future, telling us that we can hope.

We cannot live as if we had no history, no limits. Interestingly enough, in some highly skilled research conducted in the early 1970s on encounter groups, it was found that a high percentage of time in those groups was spent on personal histories, even though the leaders maintained theoretically that such should not be the case. Those groups also were the ones that seemed to lead to healthy growth in the individual members. They had dealt with more than one time perspective and apparently made better gains than those in more rigidly present-moment-oriented groups. (Lieberman, Yalom, and Miles, *Encounter Groups: First Facts.*)

When consulting with or making a referral to another

helping professional, explore the time perspective utilized. Is there a willingness to take *all* these orientations—past, present, and future—into account? Or is there a more exclusive devotion to one of them?

THE VALUE OF THE SELF

In much of the human potential movement there is heavy commitment to the welfare and value of the self. "Self-fulfillment," "the autonomy of the self," "self-esteem," and "taking responsibility for the self" are only a few of the phrases that occur with regularity in the literature. One is not encouraged to become a hermit or recluse, but strong encouragement is given to the importance of the self over against other obligations, allegiances, etc.

While exaggerated too much in some critiques of the human potential movement, the issue does place in bold relief the tension with which we live between love of self and love of neighbor. Theologically, human beings are intended to care both for self and for others. Nonetheless, at various times one focus of care has been emphasized over the other. Distorted interpretations of the concept of self-denial would have us believe that we should never give attention to ourselves and our development. In some arenas of the human potential movement we see a trend toward other-denial, usually put in a sophisticated, rational, and logical affirmation about the importance of persons "taking responsibility" for themselves and extricating themselves from dependency and paternalism.

Not a repudiation, but an added dimension, is in order as a theological response to both these extremes. Taking responsibility for oneself in terms of gratification and growth can be an affirmation of freedom. It is freedom only if there is an accompanying commitment of concern for and willingness to "stay with" other persons in *their* experiences and growth.

The freedom that takes all the perspectives into a holistic conception of humanness will move beyond the self as the source of value and meaning. There will be no heavy burden of having to prove or "making ourselves" whatever we believe ourselves to be. Rather, the source for value and meaning will be external, grounded in the God who created us and who charges us to love one another and ourselves as he has loved us. Such a commandment points out the importance of faithfulness to self and neighbor *according to a concept of humanness revealed* (external to the self) in Scripture upon which our theology is based.

When consulting with or making a referral to another helping professional, listen carefully for the values placed on self and neighbor. Is there concern for the primary relationships in which the patient or client is involved? Is there concern that those other persons receive help? Will the directions of the helping process aim at helping the person to grow in self-care *and* caring for others? Is the view of human nature one that takes responsibility to relationships as seriously as responsibility to the self?

THE VALUE PLACED ON RATIONALITY

How much value do we assign to the intellect, or rationality, in the helping and growing process? In the careful diagrams of transactional analysis, the high emphasis on the importance of feedback in groups, the rational-emotive therapy of Albert Ellis, and the reality therapy of William Glasser there is high priority placed on insight. The assumption is that insight leads to change.

In a fascinating study to which I have referred earlier (Lieberman, Yalom, and Miles, *Encounter Groups: First Facts*), the individuals who demonstrated and maintained growth were those who engaged in reflection, "cognitive learn-ing," as the authors described it. These people, after an experience that was emotionally charged, *reflected* on what had happened, what effects came from it, and *then* made decisions about what they were going to do on the basis of what they had learned about themselves. This reflection seemed to occur more frequently in groups in which the leader demonstrated a dimension of caring through the pro-cess, regardless of the theory subscribed to. Those caring leaders also tended to be people who were more firmly attached to a theory, or set of beliefs, about what was hap-pening. Reflection, incidentally, was a dimension that most of the leaders either had not mentioned or had given low priority in their scale of "mechanisms conducive to change."

Our intellect, our human propensity to seek to under-stand, shows itself as crucial in our growth. Note that the changes came in those individuals who employed *both* emo-tion and rationality in their process. The message lends confirmation to the holistic concerns that come from our theology. We are persons who are both emotional and cogni-tive, both limited and gifted, concerned for both self and others. But we are also easily seduced into an either-or mentality about those characteristics. Health, however, emerges when we can avoid such distortions. And part of the health comes from our submitting ourselves to an external authority, a system of belief, that reminds us of who we are.

When you make a referral or consult with other helping professionals, watch for the presence or absence of such a holistic perspective. Are they willing to use multiple re-sources for understanding? Do they use their heads as well as their hearts? Do they have proper regard for the com-plexity of human beings, or do they try to reduce human nature to the confines of one "quick and easy" theoretical system?

REFLECTION

Gain familiarity with two or three helping theories or approaches. Devise your own method for comparing their views of human nature with the ones to which you subscribe theologically. Once you have gone through such a process, the study of various contexts for pastoral care will be more fruitful for you because alternate approaches will come to mind.

7
The Developmental Perspective

Generally referred to as "developmental psychology," this discipline is a perspective rather than a psychology. Genetics, pediatrics, and adult medicine are involved, as well as the psychological and social sciences. One of the attractive features about it is its interdisciplinary interest, including the contributions made by ministry.

Based on the assumption that individuals and groups, when healthy, move through a definable growth process, the approach seeks to describe the *stages*. The descriptions, regularly subject to refinement, serve as a helpful indicator of "expected" issues for a person in life's journey. Discovery that a person or group varies significantly from the normal stages can serve as a warning signal that attention is needed.

This approach fits nicely with our earlier theological commitments about development and responsiveness in human nature. We *believe* that human beings grow. This approach provides evidence of the growth, as well as useful information for evaluating the growth we see. While we do not limit ourselves to these observations as the final criteria for health or abnormality, they serve us in our continuing reflection on human nature and the concrete situations in which we find ourselves.

Individuals and groups move through predictable and ordered stages in their maturation. Successful completion of those stages results in healthy adjustment, satisfaction in the completion of the appropriate tasks, preparation for future tasks, and an attitude toward oneself and the world that is conducive to continued healthy growth. This assumption, as presented here, fits closely with that of Robert Havighurst, who is commonly credited with formulation of the developmental principle.

This chapter will survey various writers and applications of their developmental approaches. Their usefulness to us in ministry will then be evaluated, and suggestions for that use will follow.

GROWTH AND INDIVIDUALS

Erik Erikson and the Development of the Individual

An artist early in life, Erik Erikson painted portraits of children. No doubt that artistic interest in understanding his subjects, combined with encounters with Freud in Vienna, led him into child psychoanalysis. Never conventional in his practice, he always insisted on going into the homes of his patients and having dinner with their families. Out of that fascinating and sensitive background Erikson came to be regarded as the foremost scholar and writer on the developmental perspective.

The epigenetic principle defined by Erikson gives us the most succinct picture of his observations about the development of persons. He views the personality as having a unified ground plan. The parts of that plan have times of special emphasis, resulting in the formation of a functioning whole. In other words, the personality has a process of growth through which it moves. Normal movement through those stages results in what we would regard as health, and those stages can be identified. His use of the term "ascendancy" tells us that all the stages are present throughout life, but each has its special era, a time when the personality focuses on that developmental issue in particular.

Especially helpful is Erikson's identification of these stages in terms of dynamic tension. A person does not experience growth in terms of neat, positive goals to be sought after. Instead, there appears to be a polarity. In fact, these seeming opposites work together to bring about a balance of ability and perception. For the individual to move too far toward either of the major constituents in a particular stage results in distortion and impaired future development. Those distortions fit well with the concepts of limitation and sin that we have discussed in our theological approach to human nature. Bear in mind that this is a *descriptive* approach to human nature. Our theological approach concerns itself with the value of life and its intended nature. The psychological approach concerns itself with the observable, with what can be described.

Erikson's Eight Stages of Growth

Building layer upon layer, according to his epigenetic principle, Erikson describes eight basic stages through which a normal individual moves during the maturation process.

The first of these, infancy, is described as the stage of *basic trust versus mistrust.* A baby, completely dependent on others after birth, quickly begins to learn who and what can be trusted. Associations begin to develop between particular smells, sounds of voices, touch, and the pleasure or lack of satisfaction that comes with them. Is the world generally responsive? Unaffected? Or is the world unpredictable? One might question the value of mistrust in this schema, but who of us would consider it realistic to learn that *everyone* can be trusted? The child, even at this young age, begins to develop some discrimination about who and what to trust and mistrust. Significant for our interests is Erikson's belief that hope, as a human virtue, has its beginnings here in infancy and is formulative for all the later stages.

Before the first year of life has come to an end, a second stage comes into ascendancy, the stage of *autonomy versus shame and doubt.* Movement and exploration are taking place. Crawling is active, and walking is not far behind. Fascinating objects are to be seen everywhere, and now the will of the child comes into conflict with the will of the parent. And will is the second of the human virtues that have beginnings in infancy and childhood. *Will*ingness to exercise free choice and self-restraint in my human experience is focal during this era. Certainly, a child doesn't think of all this in such rational terms, but learning is taking place about what things can be done independently, what things reveal limits to my ability, and what things earn severe displeasure from people who matter. Self-confidence is desirable, but so is awareness of limits. Too much experience of shame contributes to future experiences of worthlessness and lack of will. Too much autonomy results in future acts of will that are inconsiderate of personal danger or the rights of others.

Initiative versus guilt, the third of Erikson's observed stages, normally occurs during the preschool era. Speech has developed; walking is routine; ambition and initiative are being born. Now the child has sense enough to know that "if I try to take the plate off the table while Mom is in the room, I'll never make it. So, I'll wait until she leaves the room!" Purpose, the next of the human virtues, is becoming a part of the child's makeup. The capacity to evaluate which goals to pursue and which ones to avoid because of their effect on self or others is emerging. I begin to control myself rather than assume that control must always come from the outside. Too much of a sense of guilt, however, may leave a person in constant fear of committing an error, so much so that there is no initiative, no ability to act at all.

With the arrival of school age, latency, the stage of *industry versus inferiority* ascends. Competence is the virtue that comes into primary focus. There is enough coordination, muscle control, and conceptual ability that the child can engage in many creative tasks, sometimes to the dismay of parents. Teachers are also primary figures in all this, as very strong concepts of self in terms of ability and limitations are formed. Consciousness of what is allowed for boys and girls, whites and blacks, etc., rises strongly during this period. And if race, sex, or class seems to determine what I am allowed to do, why bother to develop individual skills and abilities?

Adolescence is the time to deal with *identity versus role diffusion*. Who am I? This stage was discussed briefly in Chapter 4 on the identity formation of the minister. While experiments went on about what I could *do* in the previous stage, now the experiments focus on who I *am*. Relationships are examined, for they are the observable evidence of work being done with the virtue of *fidelity*. To whom and to what will I be faithful? "Experiment" is a special term for this age. Permanent commitments are not likely, except by mistake. Data are being gathered to be used in making permanent commitments later. Commitments being considered have to do with marriage, job, values, and other places of primary investment for the self.

Chronological age means less and less with the advent of the stage of adolescence. The formation of identity, for instance, may take years beyond the teens. American culture has been characterized as prolonging adolescence because education takes longer and longer, accompanied by multiple options in terms of relationships and careers from which a person must choose.

Assuming that a sense of self emerges, the next stage involves *intimacy versus distantiation or self-absorption.* Once my own identity is reasonably clear, I then become able to share that identity with others without fear of losing my own. Commitments are made, and now mutuality and sharing can become the focus. To be faithful to someone during adolescence carried the threat of being absorbed. In this stage of young adulthood, assuming that personal identity is reasonably clear, defensiveness becomes less necessary. The capacity to love another person ascends, caring about another almost as much as for myself. Of course, there is always the possibility that I will choose to become self-absorbed and be committed only to myself. Balance is again to be worked for. Intimate relationships, accompanied by responsible caring for myself, are the marks of health.

With the establishment of healthy relationships within or outside of marriage, *generativity versus stagnation* comes into ascendancy. Stability provided by wholesome relationships enables a person to become more committed to the world and to service. "Care" is the term used by Erikson as the virtue in this stage. A healthy sense of self, accompanied by healthy, intimate, and trusting relationships, equips me and frees me to be giving and astute in my work. My work becomes more than an activity, and my concerns move beyond just getting the job done. *Being* and *doing* blend into a generative existence, occasionally stimulated by boredom and uncertainty.

Integrity versus despair emerges in Erikson's system as the last of the adulthood stages. Experience and the shaping of the earlier stages result in wisdom or a sense of despair and disgust. The virtue of this era is wisdom, the perception that no one can accomplish all that was hoped for. Integrity is the reassurance that comes from a knowledge of having been faithful in the attempts and accomplishments that were made. In old age there can be a new appreciation for parents and children, even though they had their faults. Now death can be faced without overwhelming dread. The wisdom of old age is what leads grandparents to be so much more accepting of children than are parents. The years have contributed to more realistic expectations. This is one reason for the old joke that grandparents and grandchildren get along so well because they have a common enemy!

The Usefulness of Erikson's Stages

Developmental descriptions of the growth of individuals help us as pastors to evaluate our own expectations of people who come to us. The stages give us particular points to watch for as we hear the histories of people. Many couples marry, for instance, during their late teens or early twenties. More often than not the stage of identity versus role confusion was still in ascendance for one or both of them. They mistook an experiment in fidelity for the real thing and committed themselves to each other in too permanent a way. Intimacy was not yet a possibility for one or both of them because the identity, the sense of self, was not yet focused. Divorce becomes more understandable with this knowledge, even though we may have discomfort with the idea of divorce. Knowledge about the differing characteristics of the stage of adolescence and that of young adulthood gives us important clues to watch for in premarital counseling.

Many women's concerns current in our culture reflect the poor job done in helping women during the stage of industry versus inferiority. Many were taught that home skills were the *only* acceptable possibility for them. On the other hand, men have been taught too often that home skills were not permitted for them, and the pleasures of child care or cooking were labeled as "unmasculine," depriving them of skills. Some literature points out that women are often rushed toward the young adulthood concerns with intimacy and then halted in their development. Men are rushed past the development of intimacy skills and expected to be "generative" without the stabilizing force of healthy relationships to nurture them. (Cf. Jean Baker Miller, *Toward a New Psychology of Women.*)

Knowledge of developmental stages helps us to find the "language" that is most appropriate when dealing with an individual. To talk to an eight-year-old exclusively in terms of how he or she "feels" about things, for instance, ignores the normal stage of development for that child. What he or she can "do" is more important. To try to "force" an elderly person to go through careful analysis of the emotional components of a present relationship may not be nearly as vital as joining with them in "remembering" some things and what they learned about life and themselves.

Other sources of developmental stages are available. *The Seasons of a Man's Life,* by Daniel J. Levinson, for instance, is a careful study of the adult stages of men. Gail Sheehy's popular book *Passages* is a reasonable and readable synopsis of much developmental research and findings.

Familiarity with the developmental approach makes communication with most mental health professionals possible. The field is so widely known and accepted that few people do not have some familiarity with it.

Lawrence Kohlberg and the Moral Development of Individuals

As developmental approaches have blossomed, more refinement in the study of the individual has taken place. Kohlberg, for instance, has studied the development of values in persons. Because of our own concern with values and beliefs in the process of growth, his work is of interest to us.

Kohlberg's Six Stages of Moral Development

Kohlberg's work generally divides the moral development of individuals into three phases, each containing two stages. The basic concern is the perception of right and wrong behavior and the sources for making value judgments.

The *preconventional phase*, for instance, is characteristic of most children in the age range of four to ten. "Goodness" or "badness" is tied very specifically to behavior. In the first stage of this phase the orientation is toward negative consequences. I act as I do in order to avoid getting punished. The second stage of this preconventional phase moves toward more positive thinking. I do what I do in order to have my needs met. A shift from a punishment orientation to one interested in rewards is noted. Illustrative of these characteristics was my own daughter, who was asked if she would lie about her age in order to get into a movie at half price. I asked her why she would tell the truth. "Because," she said, "they would put me in jail if I told a lie!" There you see orientation toward punishment. A few years later, I told her the same story, asked what she would do and got the same answer. The reason had changed, however, "The people would be so proud of me for telling the truth that they would let me in free." Note the first orientation to punishment and the later developing orientation to reward.

The *conventional phase* arises around the age of ten or eleven. Behavior is still important, but the *intention* behind the behavior becomes more crucial in any judgments about good and bad action. "I didn't *mean* to" is viewed as an excuse for anything. In the latter stage of the conventional period, fixed rules and order become more important. Everyone must be treated the same. Asked an ethical question about euthanasia, for instance, a child would oppose it or support it in terms of whether everyone should be treated or given that opportunity. Individual circumstances carry little weight.

With the evolution of the *postconventional phase,* which never emerges for many, more autonomous decisions can be made. Individual circumstances are to be considered, and principles become more important than rules. The relativity of values and opinions is perceived, and more debate is encouraged and valued in making ethical decisions. In the latter stage of this phase, conscience and personal decision-making according to self-chosen ethical principles is respected.

The Usefulness of Kohlberg's Stages

As with the Erikson stages, this system helps us in evaluating and choosing a frame of reference for dealing with people. Children, for instance, could not be expected to understand a conversation about ethical principles. To attempt conversations with an adult devoted to law and order about conscience and civil disobedience ends in frustration on both sides. A woman who is wrestling with a decision to divorce and wants to know whether the Bible says it is right or wrong will have difficulty with an answer that talks about conscience, internal understanding, and God's forgiveness.

Kohlberg points out that people do not seem able to understand concepts more than one stage beyond their current orientation. As we perceive where a person is, we may choose to use language one step beyond that stage in the hope of leading the person in moral development.

Some writers have criticized Kohlberg for being too simplistic in his stages. There needs to be more caution before blindly pushing people to move to the "next stage." Bear in mind, however, that his work is descriptive and does not necessarily mean that these stages "ought" to be this way. We must still make our own value judgments about what we want to encourage or discourage in the development of people for whom we care.

GROWTH AND GROUPS

Developmental specialists recognize that growth processes take place in groups as well as in individuals. Research goes on in the development of business groups, administrative teams, therapy groups, and families. Times of testing, times of retreating, and times of trusting emerge in the life of relationships. Those times are affected by the individual stages of development. Therefore, the stages are not as neatly defined. However, this section will present some of the work that has gone on.

Evelyn Duvall and Family Development

Long respected in the field of family research and development, Evelyn Duvall published a book, *Family Development,* many years ago that has remained valuable. Note that her work is concerned with the development of the family, not the married couple. Her stages are dependent on the ages of children. If there are no children, if the couple remain childless, then the description has little validity.

Before listing the stages through which families move, Duvall observes that there are common tasks to be dealt with, renegotiated or, to the detriment of the relationship, ignored. Each of these tasks is affected by each stage of the family's pilgrimage.

Listed briefly, the tasks include:

1. Physical provision of facilities. Where do we live, and is it satisfactory to us? Decisions about place, style, amount of room, and whether it is apartment, house, condominium, are all affected and discussed at each stage of development.

2. Finances. Who is going to work? Are we making enough money? How do we manage, and who will manage the money that we have?

3. Assignment of responsibilities. Who empties the gar-

bage? Who takes care of the children? Who manages the money? Are there role steieotypes, and do they work?

4. Attention to sexual and physical relationship. How do we express affection to each other? Is it enough? Is it sensitive to both persons' needs and sensibilities? Is it always aimed toward intercourse? What needs for privacy do we need to discuss and establish?

5. Systems of intellectual and emotional communication. What do we need to talk about? What common and differing interests do we have? What new interests are developing and how do they impinge on the other persons in the family? How do we keep in touch about our interests, our feelings, our hopes and dreams?

6. Contacts with relatives and extended family. How welcome are our relatives in our home, and can they come without advance notice? What visits will we make? What part will they play in the lives of the children?

7. Contact with the world, friends, etc. Do we have enough mutual friends? How much do we want to go out, become involved in community activities, do volunteer work? What if we don't like each other's friends?

8. Philosophy of life. What values mean most to each of us? What religious needs and beliefs do we act on, and how much should we expect other members of the family to share them with us?

As you can see, each of these tasks is weighty. And each of them will obviously vary from stage to stage, some remaining unchanged, some changing radically. Unfortunately, if they are not talked about with regularity, someone wordlessly dictates for the family how the tasks will be handled. Emotional separation can occur between family members from one stage to the next, and it may not be recognized until serious differences have set in.

The stages themselves are built on the age of the children, specifically on the age of the *oldest* child. An entire system is affected every time one individual makes a shift in age or developmental circumstance.

The Usefulness of Knowledge About Family Stages

Add the individual and familial developmental issues that are taking place and you see the immense stress with which a family must cope. Our knowledge of these stages alerts us to educational programs and the value of carefully timed visits.

In the first church I served, I used the list of Duvall's tasks to compose a list of times when the minister might be of help. After publishing that list in the weekly newsletter, I was overwhelmed with the number of people who called saying that they needed to talk about one of those issues. On another occasion I advertised the beginning of a group in the church designed to deal with communication in families. My assumption had been that those most interested would be spouses who had been married from five to ten years. On the first evening, five of the six couples who appeared were couples whose last child had left home. They wanted to give attention to their "new estate" so that the tasks would not be neglected and thus damage their enjoyment of their living together again without children.

Knowledge of these times of transition enables us to visit, to inquire, and to take initiative in the lives of families in our churches. Often they will not call, but they will respond quickly if we call them.

DEVELOPMENTAL PROCESS AND THE PASTOR

The principles of initiative and faithfulness guide us in our selection of other supporting disciplines to help us in our pastoral tasks. Developmental process provides us with concrete indicators to watch for as we go about our task. Furthermore, it provides us with a language to use in our consultation with other helping professions.

Three major points of usefulness include, first, helpfulness in *evaluating* the persons and groups with whom we work. When we observe something out of accord with a normal developmental process, we can exercise initiative to find out if something serious is taking place. Developmental understanding aids us in evaluating individual situations and in deciding what visits and contacts seem more important than others.

Part of our evaluation will depend on developmental information that gives us clues about deterioration or recovery. For instance, there are stages of deterioration through which relationships go if they are coming apart. Recognition of these signals will help us to understand how severe a relationship problem is. Those stages are discussed in Chapter 13.

A second use of developmental process stages is in determining *strategy.* Not only are we able to recognize something that is not within the normal bounds of development but we also have some understanding of the language and concepts to use as we attempt to render care with propriety. A small child whose parents are divorcing cannot understand conversation about whether it is "best" for the parents because of the hurt they cause each other. All he or she can understand is the personal hurt involved in what is going to happen. For a young teenager to listen to conversation about intimacy, the meaning of the word is "sex." Understanding intimacy as commitment has not ascended yet. Because of those different capacities and foci of attention in different stages, we must plan what we shall talk about and the language we shall use when taking initiative.

Third in our list of uses is *proper referral.* As we detect issues in people's lives that call for attention, our understanding of developmental issues will help us to choose a proper referral. Further, it helps us to provide understandable information to the professional to whom we refer. There are multiple resources to be found in most communities now, and they are often specialized. Our knowledge of those specialties must be developed so that as we come upon difficulties we will know where help is most readily available.

REFLECTION

Using the individual stages of Erikson, perhaps with further reading, reflect on your own stages and think back on specific experiences that may have affected your growth in each of them. For instance, do you regard yourself as a very trusting person? What are some of the situations that trigger mistrust in you? Are there associations in your past that help you to understand all this? The same sort of questions can be asked about autonomy, shame, initiative, inferiority, identity, intimacy, etc. Where do you see yourself now in terms of the "times of ascendancy"?

If you are married, you may want to think as well about the tasks discussed in the section on Duvall. How communicative are you with your spouse and your children on these issues? Depending on the ages of your children and the length of your marriage, are you satisfied with those levels of communication? If you have children, are they interfering with the level of intimacy you want with your spouse? On the other hand, maybe the relationships with your children have been neglected and issues are dealt with *only* with your spouse. These materials can provide healthy foundations for "time out" family discussions.

Finally, give some thought to how you might use this information in your ministry. What things have you already seen in relationships, conversations, etc., that this material helps you to understand better? Perhaps you remember times of talking about an issue with someone who never seemed to understand. Was the stage of development a part of the reason?

After you have finished your reflection process (which is a developmental method, you know!), let's move on to some of the other disciplines of support.

For Further Reading

Boisen, Anton T. *The Exploration of the Inner World.* Willett, Clark & Co., 1936.

Duvall, Evelyn. *Family Development.* 2d ed. J. B. Lippincott Co., 1962.

Erikson, Erik H. *Childhood and Society.* W. W. Norton & Co., 1963.
———. *Identity and the Life Cycle.* International Universities Press, 1959.

Gesell, Arnold, et al. *The Child from Five to Ten.* Rev. ed. Harper & Row, 1977.
———. *Youth: The Years from Ten to Sixteen.* Harper & Brothers, 1956.

Havighurst, Robert J. *Developmental Tasks and Education.* David McKay Co., 1972.

Kohlberg, Lawrence. *Adult Moral Development.* New Haven, Conn.: Religious Education Association, 1976.

Levinson, Daniel J. *The Seasons of a Man's Life.* Alfred A. Knopf, 1978.

Oates, Wayne E. *On Becoming Children of God.* Westminster Press, 1969.

Sheehy, Gail. *Passages.* E. P. Dutton & Co., 1976.

___ 8 ___
Psychotherapy

Ministers commonly see persons suffering. Frequently those who manifest physical symptoms already have placed themselves under the care of a physician. Our contact with these persons occurs as an accompaniment to the medical treatment they are receiving.

Those suffering emotional distress often present themselves to us first. These persons frequently are in need of our help in choosing a person often for short- or long-term psychotherapy as well as medication.

Referrals to psychotherapists, medical and nonmedical, may be one of our most frequent contacts with other professionals in the community. Therefore it is important that we understand what psychotherapy is, how it is practiced, who the various practitioners are, and the choices available to those practitioners in terms of technique.

WHAT IS PSYCHOTHERAPY?

Psychotherapy is aimed at the relief of some difficulty, a "healing of the spirit." Ordinarily a person comes to psychotherapy because of some felt *dis*satisfaction. The *Diagnostic and Statistical Manual of Mental Disorders* of the American Psychiatric Association defines a mental or emotional disorder as

> typically associated with either a painful symptom (distress) or impairment in one or more important areas of functioning (disability). In addition . . . the disturbance is not only in the relationship between the individual and society. (*Diagnostic and Statistical Manual of Mental Disorders,* III, p. 6)

Note that the definition does not concern itself with the *addition* or *gain* of some emotional or mental state as much as it is concerned with providing *relief* from distress or disability that is personal as well as relational. Some writers and practitioners speak of "growth psychotherapy" and would recommend psychotherapy for a person who, though not particularly unhappy, still wants to grow in sensitivity and understanding of self and others. Psychotherapy in this case still is concerned with change and is a change-oriented process.

Its body of knowledge makes psychotherapy more than ordinary conversation oriented toward change. A psychotherapist is assumed to have a broad understanding of psychology. Further, he or she should have received education in techniques and approaches that make responsible use of that knowledge. We know all sorts of people who are effective in caring for others but are not certified as therapists. They skillfully use their intuition and experience as effective tools. The psychotherapist, it is to be hoped, has such sensitivity and intuition. But in addition, that psychotherapist must have formal training and demonstrate some degree of mastery of the knowledge in the field.

Many opinions exist about effective *methods* in psychotherapy. Generally speaking, however, there are two views in common use. First, there is psychotherapy aimed toward *insight.* Psychotherapy of this type aims toward enabling the "clients" to "understand" the situations in which they find themselves. Having examined themselves and their environment carefully and made use of interpretations offered by the therapist, individuals can exercise new ways of "being" and thus be relieved of troubling symptoms or circumstances. If not relieved of the problems, they may at least gain understanding of them, and possibly some relief.

Other therapists direct their major efforts toward a second method or purpose. *Experience,* rather than understanding, is viewed as the key to change. A warm and supportive relationship provided by the therapist may serve as a positive experience, enabling the patient or client to experiment with other arenas in his or her life. Or, a powerful memory relived within the protected environment of the therapist's office may be the experience regarded as most beneficial. Experimentation with new styles of living is devised in the office and tried out between appointments. Positive or negative results from the experiment become the focus for the ongoing therapeutic conversation.

THE PSYCHOTHERAPEUTIC SPECIALTIES

In general, professional psychotherapists carry at least one of two primary sources of certification. First, academic credentials are gained by the successful completion of an accredited university graduate program. Other sources of credentials are professional associations, such as the American Psychological Association, the American Association of Pastoral Counselors, the American Association of Marriage and Family Therapists. Each of these groups establishes levels of certification with special committees to review the duration and quality of training received by an individual. For a person to have both academic and professional certification indicates a process of training in which the professional has moved through at least two periods of examination and training.

More and more states are beginning to establish licensure requirements for the practice of psychotherapy. Usually the terms are defined according to the standards of academic and professional groups within the particular state.

Psychiatry

A psychiatrist has completed medical school and at least four years of residency in the treatment of neurological and psychiatric disorders. Further, certification by the American Board of Neurology and Psychiatry should be obtained. Thus both psychotherapy and appropriate drugs may be offered to patients. There are many occasions when apparent psychological difficulties are the expression of an underlying and undetected organic disorder. When there is any suspicion of physical difficulty, a medical consultation is very much in order. The major distinction to be kept in mind about the psychiatrist is the *unique* authority to administer medicine and to direct hospital treatment. Of course, medical training also broadens diagnostic capabilities for evaluating a person in trouble.

Clinical and Counseling Psychology

The psychologist receives academic training in two primary areas. The first involves diagnosis and diagnostic testing. The Rorschach (inkblots), the Thematic Apperception Test (storytelling), intelligence tests, etc., require extensive training in the interpretation of data or responses obtained from the person being evaluated. That body of knowledge is the special domain of the clinical psychologist, and, to a lesser extent, the counseling psychologist.

The second area of special training is psychotherapy. Based on the results of testing, the fact is that the psychologist is in a unique position to design a strategy for therapy or to make recommendations to some other therapist. The area of counseling psychology was created for those psychologists more interested in the psychotherapeutic process than in the diagnostic one.

Psychiatric Social Work

More and more social workers have chosen to specialize in psychiatric, or emotional, difficulties. Long valuable in the community as referral sources because of their knowledge of programs for people with specialized problems, many social workers have found themselves able to provide the necessary counseling. Therefore, more and more academic and professional certification routes are available for them. Many work in groups in private practice, but they are found most often in clinics, hospitals, or in the offices of other specialties.

Pastoral Counseling

A pastoral counselor ordinarily has completed a degree in theological education, following it with several years of specialized training in counseling. Skills in counseling, combined with knowledge and willingness to deal directly with *values* in the therapeutic process, make them a valuable resource to the pastor. Their identity as ministers makes them an attractive option to persons who are wary about trusting themselves to a psychiatrist, a psychologist, or other mental health worker.

Marriage and Family Counselors

Other professional groups are identified by their concern rather than by their academic background and specialty. The American Association of Marriage and Family Therapists is an example. Professionals in all the specialties discussed above may belong to this organization. Their bond is a common interest in marriage and familial difficulties and dynamics. Quantity and quality of experience become standards of admission for members of various specialties.

SCHOOLS OF THOUGHT

Many of the professional groups have organized themselves around particular schools of thought about the nature of personality, etiology of emotional difficulties, or specific approaches to methodology in psychotherapy. Since they are far too numerous to cover in this chapter, our attempt is to familiarize you with some of the more commonly articulated approaches in psychotherapy at this time.

Psychoanalysis

While most psychoanalysts are physicians, there is no requirement for that to be the case. Credited for its formation as a technique or approach, Freud wrote massively about its theory and practice. The method ordinarily calls for frequent meetings between patient and therapist, often for years. While the approach is highly verbal, there is a high degree of emphasis on *reexperiencing* significant early events through the transference relationship with the therapist. The psychoanalytic approach is aimed primarily at change through understanding, although the experience is crucial to that understanding coming about in a real sense. Because of the length and expense of this type of therapy, there are very few who hold to this approach in a strict way. The research and understanding of psychoanalysis has been highly influential on many of the other approaches to psychotherapy.

Client-centered Therapy

Articulated most clearly by Carl Rogers, this approach is based on a developmental understanding of personality, accompanied by an optimism about human personality. Cautious about a moralistic approach to problem-solving, the client-centered method places responsibility on the therapist to provide warmth, positive regard, and unconditional acceptance for the client. Fostering such an atmosphere of trust provides the conditions most effective for the patient to examine self more closely, gaining understanding and courage to deal with difficulties in more healthy fashion. Rogers' approach has been one of the greatest sources for knowledge about good listening skills, especially helpful to beginning counselors. Rogers himself, if ever viewed in action, could not be characterized as passive and "nondirective." His warmth and aggression in the task of communicating genuine interest to persons under his care are remarkable and instructive.

Marriage and Family Therapy

A basic tenet of marriage and family therapy is that individuals do not become disturbed in isolation. Relationships are always involved, and the task of the therapist is to become familiar with the network, or system, of relationships in which a person lives. Such an approach results in psychotherapy involving many people. Sessions are scheduled with the family as a unit. The intent is to heighten their awareness of, and thus their desire to change, the environment in which they live and which they have created.

Marriage and family therapists will vary widely in their techniques, but they are united in their view that emotional disturbance is *inter*personal as well as *intra*personal. They are usually more active and intense in their approach than some of the other schools of thought. The concept of a system that is well-organized but unhealthy calls for an intervention on the part of the therapist that skillfully interrupts or breaks up that organization. With the interruption comes an opportunity to rebuild a system that takes on more healthy characteristics.

The Human Potential Therapies

Characterized by a high level of optimism about human nature and active therapeutic style, the human potential approaches have been very popular over the last decade. Writers such as Abraham Maslow, Gordon Allport, and Carl Rogers have been regarded as philosophical formulators of this movement.

Transactional analysis is the approach attributed to Eric Berne. It involves a conception of personality consisting of three ego states: parent, adult, and child. Transactions are the exchanges that go on between any two human beings. Knowledge of the way in which the ego states affect transactions results in teaching as a major function of the therapist who utilizes transactional analysis. The method seems most effective when used in group contexts rather than in individual therapy. The International Transactional Analysis Association has various levels of membership and certifies members from all specialties, including medicine, psychology, social work, and ministry.

Another school within the human potential therapies is that of Fritz Perls. Known as Gestalt therapy, this approach places high emphasis on intensity, and is quite distinct from Gestalt psychology. Also carried out primarily in groups, the method is aimed at helping people past "impasses" that block them from better self-understanding, contact with their feelings, and healthy relationships. Gestalt therapy does not lend itself to the specific systems that transactional analysis provides. Perls saw the intellect as a major block to the person trying to experience himself or herself emotionally. Consequently, to try to work out a "system" would impede the "process" he was trying to foster. As with transactional analysis, there are training associations and levels of certification that one may pursue in learning the methods of Gestalt.

The human potential therapies have achieved great popularity among religious groups. Many pastoral counselors have adopted their approaches and techniques. Many churches have utilized educational programs that are based on the understanding of human nature that is developed in these schools of thought. While many of the techniques are useful and frequently enjoyable, it is important to study the aims and conceptions of personality on which they are based.

The Rational/Reality Therapies

The human potential therapies illustrate commitment to teaching in some cases and absolute devotion to the importance of feelings in others. There are some schools of thought that elevate rationality as the essential feature to be worked with in therapy. Approaches such as those of William Glasser and Albert Ellis illustrate such a view.

Glasser claims *reality therapy* as the appropriate title for his approach. He points out effectively that the feelings or emotions of a person can cloud perception of what is really going on. People then respond to their distorted perception rather than to "what is." Consequently his approach devotes great time and energy to making patients or clients examine closely the *effects* of their behavior.

In like manner Albert Ellis, with his rational-emotive therapy, known as RET, presses for persons to see the irrational nature of their response to events in their lives. Ellis and his followers, then, would press clients to see the ways in which they exaggerate their problems. The exaggeration provides them with an excuse to avoid coming to terms with an issue. They remain unhappy, with the conviction that nothing can be done. Pressure to see the problem in an orderly manner and then to work out a logical approach to solving it is the method utilized.

The exponents of these approaches pride themselves on using rational and logical analysis to bring about very practical changes in people. Again, there are training centers and certification procedures available to people in various disciplines.

CHOICE OF TECHNIQUE AND EFFECTIVENESS OF THERAPY

The schools of thought and therapeutic approaches listed in this chapter are only a few of the bewildering array of therapies available. Both ministers in search of continuing education and patients in search of help can find themselves lost in trying to choose the approach that is most effective. Encouragement is available.

A variety of studies conducted over the last decade indicate that the choice of technique is not nearly as important as the level of trust in a relationship between therapist and counselee. Remember our earlier discussions about the importance of commitment to a system. While such a commitment to a school of thought on the part of the psychotherapist is important, it is an *auxiliary* to the more important ingredient of warmth and concern. Minister and therapist are only as effective in their work as they are willing to care and let that care be evident to the person whom they are serving. *If* that characteristic is there, the choice of technique then becomes a structure to keep the therapist from slipping into an approval-seeking style that puts him or her at the mercy of the patient. The school of thought aids in the understanding, the design of strategy, and the appropriate referral, when necessary. Continued study of various schools of thought keeps the therapist alert and growing, thus more effective in providing psychotherapy.

In making your choices for further learning and referral

of persons in need of help, acquaint yourself with the techniques and methods of psychotherapy. But don't limit yourself to those techniques as your final criteria. Far more important as a first order of business is to find the person who cares enough to make his or her choice of approach effective.

REFLECTION

We have commented on the bewildering array of choices that can be made if you are choosing a psychotherapeutic approach to learn or a professional person to whom to make a referral. Such selections are complicated and call for reflection. Remember that each of these approaches has been devised out of some person's or group's experience. Their work may have been with particular kinds of difficulties and called for a method that helped them to use their own personal characteristics and beliefs about human nature in the most effective way. That is a selection process that you will have to carry out as well. A technique is not effective in and of itself. It is a technique and belief system being utilized by a particular kind of person. By the same token, a person without the support of some kind of belief system and strategy remains, for the most part, ineffective in attempting to provide therapy, or relief, for other persons.

You must carry out some more self-examination. Evaluate which of these summaries of therapeutic approaches has seemed attractive to you. Read some more within that school of thought. See if it seems to fit. Then, explore some others to see what kind of conversation could go on between them and their perceptions about human nature.

Equally important is the reflection you carry out in the dialogue between your choices as to therapeutic approaches and your theological commitments and beliefs about the growth process of persons. The results will influence heavily the choices you make for yourself and others in the quest for relief from emotional difficulties.

For Further Reading

American Psychiatric Association. *Diagnostic and Statistical Manual of Mental Disorders.* 3d ed. American Psychiatric Association, 1980.

Berne, Eric. *A Layman's Guide to Psychiatry and Psychoanalysis.* Rev. ed. Simon & Schuster, 1968.

————. *Principles of Group Treatment.* Oxford University Press, 1966.

————. *Transactional Analysis in Psychotherapy.* Grove Press, 1961.

Bowen, Murray. *Family Therapy in Clinical Practice.* Jason Aronson, 1978.

Ellis, Albert. *Humanistic Psychotherapy.* Julian Press, 1973.

Fagan, Joen, and Shepherd, Irma Lee, eds. *Gestalt Therapy Now: Theory, Techniques, Applications.* Science and Behavior Books, 1970.

Glasser, William. *Reality Therapy.* Harper & Row, 1965.

Harris, Thomas A. *I'm OK—You're OK.* Harper & Row, 1969.

Koch, Joanne and Lew. *The Marriage Savers.* Coward, McCann & Geoghegan, 1976.

Rogers, Carl R. *On Becoming a Person: A Therapist's View of Psychotherapy.* Houghton Mifflin Co., 1961.

Rogers, Carl R., and Stevens, Barry. *Person to Person: The Problem of Being Human; A New Trend in Psychology.* Lafayette, Calif.: Real People Press, 1967.

Satir, Virginia M. *Conjoint Family Therapy.* Rev. ed. Science and Behavior Books, 1967.

Satir, Virginia M., et al. *Helping Families to Change.* Jason Aronson, 1976.

Stephenson, F. Douglas, ed. *Gestalt Therapy Primer.* Charles C Thomas Publisher, 1975.

9
Community Resources, Interdisciplinary Cooperation, and Referral

Psychotherapy is one major resource to which the pastor turns, but there are many other available helping professions in the public and private sectors. It is all too easy for a pastor to assume that the major difficulties presented to him or her lie in the area of emotional problems. Not so. Many mental health problems even call for resources other than or in addition to the help provided by psychotherapists.

This chapter will list some of the other major resources that are available to the pastor and suggest ways in which cooperation can be fostered. Referral is a special concern, because of the immense implications for the relationship between the pastor and the person or agency to whom the referral is made, as well as for the person being referred.

COMMUNITY RESOURCES

Regular surveys should be made of the community by any pastor. New services become available, new people offer old services, and special interests develop in the community for dealing with problems. Familiarity with all these resources is one of the most helpful services a pastor can offer. In a survey carried out by the Readiness for Ministry Project of the Association of Theological Schools, one of the major expectations that laity and other clergy had of ministers was knowledge and ability to put people in touch with resources in the community. (Schuller, Strommen, and Brekke, *Ministry in America.*)

Physicians

An ongoing relationship of trust with a primary or family practice physician in the community is of immense help to any pastor. In our visits with the sick at home and in hospitals there are diseases and reactions that we do not understand or that do not seem to fit with our understanding of what is wrong. A physician can fill us in on characteristics of an illness, effects of medication, and treatment of choice. Our observations about the patient's specific behavioral response to the progress of treatment can be valuable information for the doctor. Understandably, doctors must be cautious about discussing their treatment. Nonetheless, we can be a helpful resource for them if we are introduced by a physician friend as someone whose observations are reliable. Service is the mutual bond that aids the development of a relationship and the pursuant cooperation. We both are interested in the health of those we serve, and our joys and griefs can be shared and understood. The relationship with a physician can be more than a formal information exchange. There is the possibility of an understanding friendship that develops over time. The physician, by the nature of his or her work, is limited as to when medical service can be rendered. The patient must take the initiative. The minister, on the other hand, can take the initiative. It is a part of our calling, accepted as part of our tradition. We can thus serve as the "pusher" to see to it that a person gets medical intervention at times when she or he may have shied away from it.

Nurses

Although not trained or authorized to diagnose medical conditions, nurses have education and accumulated experience that can provide much of the information described in the section on physicians. They implement physicians' orders and carry the responsibility of staying with patients throughout the hours, days, and weeks of treatment. Caring for an ill person is an intimate relationship, and confidences are often offered to the nurse that are not offered to the doctor. Out of that knowledge of the patient, a discriminating and careful nurse can help us to plan pastoral care for the sick sensitively and make the best use of our time.

Nurses, as well as doctors, benefit from the opportunity to talk with someone about their own observations, thoughts, and feelings. We can often serve them by listening. Remember that the appearance of being busy may be a sign of personal distress. A pause for a word of greeting and inquiry may open the door for pastoral care to that person as well as the patient.

Attorneys

Persons come to pastors to discuss marriage, divorce, adoption, political and legislative issues, wills, plans for the future financial welfare of their children, property disputes, and prenuptial agreements, to name only a few. Obviously we cannot and should not answer such questions as if we were specialists in the law. Nonetheless, general familiarity with the laws of the particular state and community in which we serve enables us to alert people to the importance of seeing an attorney at appropriate times. With the abundance of lawyers available in most communities and the frequent lack of previous contact with them on the part of people we see, it is also helpful to have names we can suggest in good faith.

Legal consultation for the minister arises more often than you might think. Frequently, pastors are called on to testify in divorce and child custody hearings, to give character references for people being considered for sensitive and responsible positions, or to become involved in social issues. For our own ethical and legal integrity, it is important to have an attorney to whom we can turn when such questions come up.

Common interests in the ongoing life of the community are the bonds that pull minister and attorney together. They both are generalists in large degree, finding themselves caught up in a variety of issues and concerns in their place of residence. They can provide a valuable level of support and assistance to each other out of that common experience and interest.

Social Workers

Aid in the form of money, food, fuel, housing, clothing, information on setting up a business, welfare benefits, retirement opportunities, special care for handicapped children and adults—all these needs have to be faced regularly by the community social worker. Contact with such a person puts us in touch with a competent source of information and evaluation.

Some community needs might well be met by the church in which you are involved. At that point you can be a resource to the worker. And many such social workers will breathe a sigh of relief and gratitude upon meeting a pastor who wants to design a program of help that is *needed* and *reliable,* thus becoming an aid rather than a complication in their hectic professional lives.

Teachers

Daily, prolonged contact with children makes the teacher an unusually valuable resource to the minister. Occasions of family disturbance frequently affect a child's work in school. When caring for a couple coping with divorce, for instance, the pastor can often find out from the teacher how the situation at home seems to be affecting the child. Often a teacher's observation of sudden changes in a child's school performance is the first clue that something is wrong at home. Contact with teachers is a front-line resource for preventive maintenance on the part of the pastor. If you are known as an interested and concerned community servant, you will hear from them.

Community Mental Health Centers

Within a reasonable geographic distance in most areas of the country, community mental health centers stand as a multidisciplinary resource. With staffs composed of physicians, nurses, psychologists, community social workers, psychiatric social workers, occupational therapists, vocational counselors, and frequently chaplains, these public centers offer many forms of help to the community pastor. It is usually helpful to get acquainted with someone on the staff prior to an immediate need. That person will become more available because of the prior contact and can serve as a liaison with other staff members when necessary.

Specialty Diagnostic and Treatment Clinics

Usually centered in medical school settings, multidisciplinary clinics are available in increasing numbers to assist persons in diagnosing, understanding, and getting help for various handicaps. Children, for example, can be taken to centers that evaluate them extensively for causes of physiological and/or emotional disorders. Team treatment yields information that could not be obtained from any one specialty. Overwhelming in its complexity and thoroughness, such a center is expensive to operate but offers a level of care that is crucial to special difficulties.

Although a minister does not have access to such centers on a regular basis, it is important to know that they are there. Information about them can be obtained from some of the other helping professions. On the occasions when the pastor does come into contact with retardation, psychosis, undiagnosed major physical or emotional upheavals, or severe trauma, it is good to know such places are to be found.

Special Interest Groups

Though not in the business of offering treatment, there are many special interest groups that encourage volunteer work, raise funds, and provide educational programs around special concerns. Such national organizations as the Heart Fund and the American Cancer Society are examples.

Frequently such organizations have volunteers who visit persons experiencing the problem, and often they solicit clergy support. CanSurmount, for instance, is a program of cancer patients and families visiting newly diagnosed cancer patients and their families to help them understand what they will be going through.

Interdisciplinary Cooperation

It is important for the pastor to remember that all these specialists are not somehow better or more educated than he or she. They are resources who, for the most part, are anxious to help in a way that continues to recognize a valid role for the pastor. Furthermore, they often stand in need of pastoral care themselves. If too easily intimidated by these professionals, you miss out on marvelous opportunities to learn, to teach, and to care.

The pastor has an acquaintance with the community and a view of individuals in it that is distinctive. People will share personal confidences with a pastor about their fears, hopes, and frustrations that may not be shared in the same way with anyone else. The language of their faith may be the most expressive for them in reflecting on their condition. We have the familiarity with that language, the trust they place in us, and the ability to evaluate the healthy or unhealthy manner in which they are using their resources. That is a part of the picture that is important to the rest of the interdisciplinary team.

If we use the language of some other helping profession, we lose our usefulness by sacrificing our unique perspective. The value of knowing the languages of the other professions lies in being able to "translate" back and forth, not giving up our language in favor of theirs. Effective translating lays the ground for gaining respect and friendship to meet both personal needs and professional responsibilities.

REFERRAL

Many occasions arise in the life of the pastor when referral is in order. Perception that referral is in order and knowledge of the most effective ways to make it are an important aspect of the pastoral repertoire.

When to Refer

Too often we depend on the person we are seeing to decide whether a referral is in order. Slavish to the view that we "must help people if they are counting on us," we often become frustrated and even angry at the imposition on our time and abilities. We must have our own criteria that we utilize in making such a decision.

Time is a major consideration. Do we have the time that this person and situation seem to demand? Persons who are severely depressed, for instance, become quite demanding in terms of time both in person and on the phone. While we may feel reasonably competent to work with them, the calendar tells us otherwise. Rather than frustrate them and/or ourselves by constantly having to rush, reschedule, or become irritable, it is best, when limited on time, to refer.

Of course, our *personal limits* serve as adequate reason to refer. There are times when we are under emotional stress that limits us in the amount of emotional investment we can make in another person. We may already be seeing too many people. That is a limiting factor. We need to say, "No more!" Unless we limit the number of people we see to the number that we are emotionally capable of carrying, we do little good for any of them.

Each of us has some areas in which we feel particularly incompetent: dealing with depressed or suicidal persons, sexual conflicts, or physically attractive members of the opposite sex! Whatever the limitation of ability, it is important that we acknowledge it and make appropriate referral or seek out a supervisory arrangement to aid us in our professional development. There are many available persons in the helping professions who would agree to sit in on or listen to tapes of your counseling sessions. It is a helpful learning opportunity and provides the counselee with the benefit of two persons' help, rather than one.

Mistrust sabotages any relationship of caring or counseling. With the best of intentions you or the person coming to you for help may be uneasy or mistrusting of the relationship and where it is going. Some people just do not work well together. When such a situation exists, referral is in order for the welfare of the person seeking help. The mistrust may be in you or the other person, but if it persists, referral must be at least considered.

Less easily defined but equally important as a consideration for referral is *personal uneasiness.* Perhaps you dread the week until the conversation with that person is over. Or you find yourself preoccupied with the person to such a degree that you are unable to concentrate on your other work or on the other persons you are helping. The preoccupation may be one of anger, dread, sexual attraction, helplessness, or any of the other complex emotions we can experience. While these may not be final indicators that referral is in order, there should at least be some competent supervision. Our emotions can be very deceiving. For that reason, regular collaboration with other helping professionals is so important for us in our maintenance of effectiveness.

Someone else can do it better! Frequently the pastor is the first contact for a person who is in need of specialized treatment. Our familiarity with the other resources in the community makes us a logical place to start. Imagine the amazement of a person who hears the minister say, "Come back next week at this same time," when all that was wanted was the name of someone else to go to!

Frequently, personal friends do not want to share deeply personal material with us. They fear that our respect for them will be affected. Delicacy is important in such events, because our friendship may be the very factor that will enable us to be most valuable to them. If, on the other hand, that is not their view (or ours!), then we must willingly serve as their resource to get the help they want and need.

How to Refer

Familiarity with the helping professions and their areas of expertise is the first step in making a good referral. Picking up good literature on these various specialties and keeping current with local news are good methods for knowing what is available. That way, when a person does come to us, we have a ready reference. Don't hesitate, however, to say, "I need to do some checking," if you don't know what could be most helpful.

Establishment of personal contact with some professionals in the community is a second important preparatory step in making good referrals. Get to know a psychiatrist, a psychologist, a teacher, a lawyer, a general practitioner in medicine. As you come to know these professionals, they will be helpful in suggesting names of other trusted helpers. They will take referrals from you and trust your judgment about how soon they should see them. Your personal rapport with them will serve as a major help in getting assistance for the people who come to you.

Be frank and specific with the persons you are referring. Don't frighten them with a vague statement that they "need more help" than you can give them. Point out your limitation on time, your felt inability, your sense that they might trust someone else more, or your felt uneasiness dealing with their situation. Also, express your view of the issues that need to be dealt with. Candor, combined with sensitivity, will give them more courage and willingness to go to the professional you suggest. Also, let them know that you intend to stay in touch.

In suggesting the referral, include names of specific professionals and what you know about them. Going to someone who is known makes for an easier trip than going to someone whom even the pastor didn't seem to know! You may not be able to guarantee that your parishioners will see that person, but you will have fostered trust to accept whatever recommendation is made by the helping professional you have suggested. In other words, try to make the referral as personal as possible. The sense of being cared for will give courage.

Make specific agreements with the person you are referring about whom and when to call and what contact you would like to maintain with her or him in the future. Usually it is best for the person to call for the appointment rather than having you volunteer to make it. That phone call will be his or her own commitment to the process.

Certainly times arise in which a person is so helpless or depressed that you will need to make the appointment or even take him or her. Those times are rare, however, and the more trust you place in your parishioner to carry out this task, the more sense of hope he or she will be able to maintain.

Contact the professional to whom you are making the referral. Letters or phone calls are acceptable. Frequently the letter is preferable because it can be read at a convenient time and be kept as a source of information. Give concise but complete information on your reasons for the referral, what you have told the person to expect, and what information you would like to have from the helping professional if it is agreeable and appropriate.

If you are not already known to this professional person, supply some brief information about yourself so that you will be more of a known quantity. Ask your friend within that professional community to mention you to this person. If you do already know her or him, the contact can be much more informal.

Follow up on your referrals. Do so both with the person you refer and with the professional to whom you referred. After all, you are still a concerned party. You are that person's pastor, and the principle of faithfulness still holds. While the information you gain may be quite general, your exercise of initiative in letting your parishioner know you still care is very important.

In like manner you demonstrate your faithfulness by taking initiative with the helping party. Release of information to you may not be appropriate, but you should at least inquire. Often there will be opportunity for regular collaboration and alternating schedules of seeing the person. Furthermore, after some intensive treatment, it is helpful for that professional to know that you will be maintaining a relationship with that person.

REFLECTION

If possible, schedule an interview with some of these helping professionals to find out more about them and their interest in interdisciplinary cooperation. Reflect as well on your own degree of comfort and discomfort in making those contacts and establishing such relationships. Remember the points in the process of referral. This will be a procedure you will use many times.

For Further Reading

Mason, Robert Lee, Jr., et al. *The Clergyman and the Psychiatrist—When to Refer.* Nelson-Hall, 1978.

Oates, Wayne E., and Neely, Kirk H. *Where to Go for Help,* Revised and Enlarged Edition. Westminster Press, 1972.

Oglesby, Wm. B., Jr. *Referral in Pastoral Counseling.* Abingdon Press, 1978.

PART IV
CONTEXTS
FOR PASTORAL CARE

— 10 —
A Pastoral Approach to Stress

All of us experience stress regularly in a variety of circumstances. In fact, if we did not experience it, we would be dead! The remaining chapters will focus on specific experiences of stress. However, a general understanding of it and general approaches for dealing with it will aid us in our later reflection.

STRESS: A NORMAL PART OF EXISTENCE

Descriptions

Some descriptions identify stress with discomfort. When things interfere with our sense of stability and comfort to the degree that we try to get out of the situation, we are stressed. Such experiences are routine for us in varying levels of intensity. Another understanding of stress assumes its origin in forces outside of ourselves. Certainly no one would deny that to be true of *much* stress, but many would be quick to add that we often create our own stress. The source can be within us as well as without.

Mathematically, stress can be described as a ratio of demands to resources. When demands placed on us, by someone else or by ourselves, are greater than the resources we have or perceive ourselves to have, then we are under stress. The ratio is greater than 1. When the ratio is less than 1, when the resources are more than adequate to meet the demands, we are not under stress. The requirements can be met with energy and confidence left over. When the two are equal to 1, when resources and demands are matched in a reasonably equal fashion, we are also stressed or taxed to our limits, yet capable. The stress in such an even ratio will tend to become greater if the period of time is protracted.

Theological Perspective

Whatever description you prefer, it is important to acknowledge that stress is *a normal part of human experience.* In fact, it is often a *chosen* part of human experience. Stress can be frightening for some, exhilarating for others. It can be desperately avoided or eagerly sought out as a source for motivation. Indeed, it is often a requisite if one is to live out a life that is responsible and committed.

Theologically, stress can be identified as one of the confirming features of the limited nature of human beings. We do experience stress when facing our limits. At the same time, stress signals the possibility of developing new gifts or coping strategies which we possess as human beings. Our sinfulness may lead us to presume that stress is defeating and to be avoided or that it is a challenge which must and *surely* can be overcome. Relationships aid us most in arriving at a proper perspective on stressing events. Through a supportive community we may gain deeper understanding of stress and a healthful response to it.

In addition to our theological understanding of stress, other frames of reference are useful. Developmental perspectives, you will remember, identify specific points at which stress will occur as a normal part of living and growing. Moving through physical and psychological changes provokes stress. We are alerted to change taking place. The alert having been sounded, choices must be made, although often they are avoided, to deal with this new or challenging element in our living.

We pay attention to stress, then, because it is a normal part of our existence, and a pastoral approach takes the whole of human experience into its concern. The person, body and spirit, is a unified whole, created in the image of God and deserving of concerned and careful attention. Furthermore, stress affects relationships as well as individuals. Our commitment to the welfare of relationships requires that we give due attention to experiences of stress. Corrective and growth-producing opportunities are often possible. If not, we still give attention to those for whom stress has come and for whom there seems no possible correction or productive interpretation. We care because they too are children of God.

AN INCIDENT OF STRESS

Mrs. Goodheart is forty-one years old, married to a successful corporate executive, and the mother of three children aged sixteen, twelve, and ten. Her family background has been happy for the most part, although it was privileged enough that she seldom had to carry heavy responsibility before marrying. That has continued to be the case during her marriage of twenty-one years. Both Mr. and Mrs. Goodheart have been active in their local church, teaching in the church school program, serving as officers, giving generously to mission programs and otherwise serving as a model family to those around them. Recently, they announced proudly that Mr. Goodheart was taking on new corporate responsibilities that would require a six-week trip to South America to become familiar with the company operations there.

At nine thirty one evening, four weeks after her husband's departure, Mrs. Goodheart called her pastor at home. She was in tears. Since his leaving, she said, there had been only four letters from him, compared to ten or twelve which she had written to him. A loan from the bank had become due, and she didn't know what to do about it. Furthermore, he had failed to transfer adequate funds into her checking account, and she was overdrawn at the bank. Their car had broken down, and the mechanic said it would make more sense to sell it than fix it.

For the first time in her life, Mrs. Goodheart felt things to be out of control. Her report on the phone that night and in the pastor's office the next morning was that she had moved back and forth between helpless despair and a sense of rage. "It is ridiculous for a forty-one-year-old woman not to know how to transfer funds into a bank account or how to deal with automobile problems," she wept. "How could he do this to me? I have to rely on *his secretary* to tell me where the bank accounts are and to transfer the funds because she knows more about it and has power of attorney over the checking account." Later, she spoke of her earlier lack of interest in ever learning about all these matters. Now she wanted to change, even though it would be unsettling to her way of life.

A PASTORAL STRATEGY

Although the problems being experienced by Mrs. Goodheart may be unique to a particular set of people (namely, those who have enough money to be transferring it back and forth, etc.), in terms of the details the characteristics of the stress are common. In terms of our earlier definitions, there is the element of uncomfortable *interference,* caused by her husband's absence, in her life-style. The experience of the stress is as though it were an external stressor, and the situation places more demands on her than she feels able to handle. It could be said that she, in a way, had chosen this stress by earlier decisions not to be involved in the financial aspects of their marriage. The pastor, in this case, has been called. In other cases, the pastor might hear from a third party and have to make a decision whether to "drop by to see how things are going."

The Use of Theological Resources

Once the initial contact has taken place, the pastor is in a position to exercise initiative and faithfulness through specific use of appropriate resources. In this case Mrs. Goodheart had already begun with the resource of *confession*. Confession does not mean guilt. Rather, the word means that "admission" is taking place. She is admitting to another person what is happening to her. She wants someone to *identify* with her. She is in need of *fellowship* in the deepest sense of the word. The experience of being out of control, of helplessness, and of inability to make a decision resulted in her cry for someone else to understand. The need to confess is a need to experience community and the support that community brings. The pastor is the concrete expression of that community and is thus the one whom she called.

So the pastoral approach begins for Mrs. Goodheart with the pastor *listening* to what she is experiencing. Notice in your review of what she said to the pastor that she moved quickly to both emotional and rational evaluations of herself and her husband. That is part of the initial stage of the pastoral process which centers around confession. Persons begin to examine themselves and their primary relationships in a way that may not have occurred before. To be cared for gives freedom to persons to examine themselves and their relationships with a sense of relief, along with the discomfort. New self-understanding comes from confession that is done with integrity. Furthermore, *repentance,* the decision to change, usually results. In Mrs. Goodheart's case, she did make decisions over the coming weeks about changes she wanted to make. By the time her husband returned home, she had formulated them well and invited him to join her in talking with the pastor to find ways to implement them.

A second theological resource was useful in the process of self-examination: *prayer.* Because of the level of commitment to her faith, which was shared by her husband, prayer was a resource that could be used without discomfort or embarrassment. They used it and quiet meditation to understand themselves and their nature as human beings in a deeper and more insightful way. The use of protected time, set apart from other people and responsibilities, was useful for them and helped them evaluate the changes they wanted to make.

The theological resource of *hope* was utilized as well. They could talk about what they wanted to come of this stressful period and what seemed realistic in their plans for change. The theological conclusion for them in this case was, properly, that they did not have to remain the way they were. She could learn more and assume more responsibility in order to obtain more independence than she had before. At the same time, they agreed that they did not want to foster such independence that they would somehow lessen the sharing which they both valued. Their planning resulted in a greater sense of worth placed on each of them and on the relationship.

The pastor's responsibility in all this was to listen to the admissions, support Mrs. Goodheart as she reviewed her life, and help her to discover changes she wanted to make. At times it was important both to hear her anger and later to caution her not to allow the anger to drive a wedge in the relationship by making a decision to avoid dependence altogether. Expressed concern and interest in the relationship made it easy for Mr. Goodheart to join the conversations on his return. The belief on the part of the pastor that their relationship could be enriched served as a hopeful resource for them in their examining process.

Obviously, all cases do not turn out this nicely. The choice of a success story here is for the purpose of highlighting appropriate resources. Any pastoral approach should offer these resources to a person in stress: the opportunity to identify, or confess, the stress and thus come to a clearer understanding of it; the opportunity to verbalize repentance, or a decision to change; the faithfulness of remaining with the person through that process and offering hope through the pastor's perceptions; the affirmation that stress may be shared, distributed, throughout the community of faith, rather than having to be borne alone.

Other Helpful Resources

The pastor is not the only one who can be helpful during a stressful period. He or she symbolizes a wider community of support. Encouragement may be given to talk with other close friends during a difficult period. Churches typically have special groups who are anxious to be helpful financially or in terms of visitation, care of family members, provision of transportation, etc.

In many cases the stress may be of such intensity that other helping professionals may be of more help. Or the pastor's schedule or abilities may be limited to the degree that a referral is in order.

Much research has gone on in recent years about stress. Special forms of treatment, including instruction in relaxation techniques, have proved beneficial to numerous people. Specific changes in schedule, exercise habits, diet, job choice, etc., may be recommended after careful professional evaluation. Take advantage of these helping disciplines that are so available in most communities. They can be immensely helpful in providing information on recognition of dangerous stress and healthy ways of coping with it.

REFLECTION

Begin to think about stressful experiences in your own life and the function that stress served in your own development. Which ones were growth-producing? Which ones have left negative effects that are still difficult for you? What accounts for the differences? Was it the stress itself or the way you coped?

Use what you have learned about yourself and your experiences with stress to design your own pastoral strategy for helping persons undergoing such experiences. Then move on to the chapters of this part that deal with specific forms of stress.

11

A Pastoral Approach
to Loss and Grief

Being visited by her pastor six weeks after her husband's death, the fifty-year-old widow reported: "I went downstairs yesterday to wash his clothes to give to the Salvation Army. When I picked them up, I just began to smell them. I stood there for a long time and rubbed them against my face and smelled them. It is the only contact I had left with him. Is there something wrong about my needing to do that so badly?"

Her description and her question pose issues that a sensitive pastor faces regularly. Experiences of loss, whether death or unemployment or poor health or a child leaving home for school, are regular in daily living. People grieve over those losses. At the same time they wonder about the "normality" of their grief. They need both permission to grieve and assurance that they are doing it "right."

Loss and grief traditionally have been the domain of the pastor. He or she is called when death is feared or has occurred. The pastor is called when major illness "takes away" the sense of security, stability, and/or confidence of a person and family. When loneliness, the loss of a sense of belonging, becomes overwhelming, the pastor is called by the person or those who know of the person's loneliness. Loss and grief seem to call for presence. The pastor represents the presence of the community of faith and of God.

Many times loss occurs and there is no apparent grief. That, too, raises concerns. Sometimes the person who has suffered the loss and is not experiencing the grief is the one most concerned. "What is wrong with me? I ought to be upset, and I'm not." Or the phone call comes: "I'm worried about Tom Jones. His wife died last week, and he is already back at work as if nothing happened. Isn't something abnormal about that?" To care for those who are grieving, the pastor must have knowledge about grief, familiarity with available resources, and the ability to design a strategy for the ongoing care of the people involved.

THE GRIEF PROCESS

Writers in the developmental perspective inform us about the commonality of experience in people suffering loss. Autobiographies often provide vivid accounts of the process of adjustment to loss. Our own biblical heritage provides rich information. Recent study within the fields of medicine and psychology provides clinical documentation of what biblical writers and existentialist authors have told us for centuries.

Biblical Resources

One of the most helpful places to turn in the Bible for understanding grief is the Old Testament book of Psalms. No fewer than sixty-one of the one hundred and fifty psalms are categorized as psalms of lament by the New Oxford Annotated edition of the Revised Standard Version of the Bible.

Careful reading of these expressions of lament yields a common pattern with countless variations. Psalm 22 is a good example. As with most of the laments, the opening verses are a cry for help. Then the writer moves on with rhythmic movement among agonizing descriptions of the illness, apparent moments of relief, and meditation on God's promises. Even when God's faithfulness is questioned, the author continues to address the words to him. The expressions of pain seem to diminish and the expressions of hope increase until the psalm ends with a hymn of praise.

Several things are noteworthy about lament, or the expression of grief, from reading these psalms. First, there is no attempt to disguise the excruciating misery of the person or group that is suffering. Common acknowledgment seems implicit about the normality and acceptability of giving vent to those feelings. Second, the words are always addressed to another. The suffering does not exist only in private. In fact, the articulateness of some sufferers is recorded for the use of other sufferers who need effective words to give vent to their own unhappiness. It is important to say it and be heard. Third, there is a rhythm in the experience. Overwhelmed at one moment, the writer seems to experience moments of relief at others. Fourth, memory serves as a healing resource. Writers recall previous difficult experiences and God's faithfulness in them. That serves as comfort in the present. Then praise is offered with conviction that such comfort will come again.

Familiarity with these laments and other biblical resources such as The Book of Job are valuable for our own instruction about the nature of grief. They are valuable as well for those to whom we minister and who need a sense of being understood. Carefully selected passages of Scripture for them to read during reflective moments may be one of the most valuable resources we can offer to them.

Psychological Findings

Studies of grief in recent history begin in the late 1930s. Following the Boston Cocoanut Grove fire in 1942, the studies of Erich Lindemann and his colleagues led to the identification of stages of grief, unhealthy reactions, and specific suggestions as to the best care of persons suffering from grief. Even more recently the studies of Elisabeth Kübler-Ross have received popular attention among those working with terminally ill patients. Further work has been done on understanding grief among children.

The Stages of Grief

While each study has its own nomenclature and numbers of stages in the grief process, the following discussion reasonably incorporates the major findings.

First, upon learning of a death or major loss, the person is *shocked.* While that first phase may last only seconds, its major feature is numbness. The body desperately gets into a state of readiness for what is to come. For some, the shock may take the form of apparent difficulty in hearing or disbelief: "Would you say that again? I don't think I understood you." Other people literally will turn and run, attempting to "get away from" this bad news. Fainting is common. Or some will stand, openmouthed and silent, for a few seconds.

Second, the impact of the loss strikes and there is a sense of being bowled over by what has happened. That sense of being overcome often *alternates* with periods of relief. The grief seems to come in waves, alternating between intense emotion and a return of the sense of numbness. Gradual incorporation, or acceptance, of the reality can almost be observed by anyone watching. Note the similarity between this clinical description of the grief process and the rhythmic moving back and forth between despair and hope of the psalmists.

As the speed of the alternations between intensity and relief increases, there comes a period of time in which the *intensity* seems to remain. It is almost as if the person is "ready" to accept the full impact of the loss. The period of time in this stage of intensity varies widely depending upon the nature of the loss, the quality of the relationship, other sources of emotional support that are available, etc. Furthermore, the experience will vary. Tears are not the only expression. Anger is a frequent occurrence, as is agitation and constant movement. Some persons will want constant company during this period. Others will want privacy with little interference.

The fourth stage seems to repeat the second. Having passed through the period of greatest intensity, the person has *intermittent* times of strong emotion and lengthening phases of relief. Perhaps the difference between the second and fourth stages is the function being served. Stage two is preparing the person to accept the full reality. Stage four is allowing the person to move past absorption with the loss into a period of adjusting and rebuilding.

Often it is difficult to distinguish with clarity between the first four stages. They blend into each other and move along with amazing rapidity. The fifth stage, however, lasts much longer, if indeed it ever ends. It is the stage of *remembering*. The person becomes more able and anxious to recall important, as well as insignificant, moments in the relationship with the person or object of loss. Memories of dating, trips taken together, promises made to each other, come to mind, and the person wants to talk about them. After retirement, a person wants to talk about the "early days" or remember critical moments and laughable mistakes made in his or her life. Now is the time for much talking, and it is important *not* to try to steer the person away from such talking. It is a sign of healthy movement toward the last stage.

Reinvestment is my preferred term for this sixth and final stage of the grief process. Some prefer to call it acceptance, but that is too passive a term for me. The person moves out and begins to find new places, activities, and people to meet the needs formerly met by the lost person or object. That which has been lost will not be replaced. There will not be someone or something to meet those needs in the same way. But the needs still exist and call for attention. New work, new relationships, new activities, are signs of reinvestment —signs of hope that life will go on rather than remain static.

Grief in Children

Children grieve, too. Adults often forget that. One of the most confusing things for children is to see everyone upset and grieving, then be shuffled off with a baby-sitter until everyone gets back to normal. They don't know what happened and are left with many fears about it. Further, they may then notice that someone is missing and be told that the person has "gone away on a long trip." Sooner or later they will learn that they have been told a lie, and mistrust remains with them about what other important things they have not been told.

Certainly young children do not understand death. Nonetheless, their experiences with separation, responses to bodily injuries, stories about people being "taken away," and events such as the one described above form lasting imprints that will affect the way they handle grief.

Abnormal Grief Reactions

Unfortunately, people do not always go through the normal process. They become "stuck" and often are in need of help. Some of the signs to watch for include a delay or postponement of grief following a significant loss. There may be no crying or anger or even evident acknowledgment of what has happened. People have been known to go for years before coming to terms with a major loss. That acknowledgment is often triggered by some other event, and the load becomes too much.

Watch, too, for exaggerated reactions to the loss. Continued agitation, refusal to leave the house, nondiminishing and furious hostility about past events, failure to take responsibility for financial matters, children, job, etc.—all these may signal a failure to be moving through the experience to reinvestment. Grief can often lapse into depression which maintains itself for months and years after the actual loss.

Any of the early stages discussed under normal grief can, if prolonged, become a signal of abnormal grief. Persons may remain in the stage of shock, denying by their behavior that the loss has taken place. Or they may remain in the stage of intensity, remaining overwrought and unable to function for months or even years.

TWO INCIDENTS OF GRIEF

An eighteen-year-old boy in college received a phone call at 12:30 A.M. that his mother had died suddenly of a heart attack. He hung up the phone, calmly said to a person in the hall, "My mother just died," and returned to his room. After sitting in his chair for a few minutes and looking out of the window, he began to weep. Friends were beginning to hear the news and gathered outside his room, but he kept the door locked and refused to respond to their calls. He wept for a time, then began to pack his suitcase, then would sit down again in tears, unable to continue his packing. When he finished packing, he unlocked his door and felt able to accept the consolation of his friends.

Then, unable to sleep, he drove all night to get home. The alternation continued between having to stop because of his tears and then being able to drive. Upon arriving home, he saw his father, burst into tears, and then felt pretty nonfunctional for the next two or three days. The funeral was very difficult. He returned to school, visited with the college chaplain from time to time over the next few months and talked about memories of his mother, times enjoyed and times regretted. He noticed over the next few years that he became more interested in visiting with the parents, especially the mothers, of his friends when he would go home with them to visit.

Though described in very capsule form, the above scenario is typical of a normal grief process. There is obvious pain, but the stages can be seen as they develop.

In another case, a family of five away from home on vacation was involved in a critical accident. The mother and two older children were killed. The father and his six-year-old daughter were hospitalized. She was not harmed seriously but was kept in the hospital for a time only because there was no other place for her to stay. She wept continuously, asking for her parents. The father, confined to his bed, refused to let the daughter be brought to him. He had been told of the deaths of his wife and the two other children. Angrily he accused the hospital staff of lying to him, and he continued to refuse to see his daughter.

Finally the chaplain of the hospital, after three days, came on his regular visit to the father and said: "Look, I am tired of having to try to convince your daughter that she has a father. If you are her father, why won't you be one?" With that, he called the nurse to bring in the daughter. When the father looked at her, he burst into tears, and they began to weep together over the loss of their family.

While the approach may seem drastic, it was carried out after interprofessional collaboration and agreement that the father was "stuck" in the denial stage. For his sake and the sake of the daughter whose anxiety was so intense, a forceful intervention had to be made to "bring him along" in his grief. Ordinarily, such a push would not take place so soon. People need their own pace at moving through these stages. But watchfulness is necessary, along with consultation in the professional and lay community, about the best ministry to persons in grief.

A PASTORAL STRATEGY

As we keep in mind the prior understanding we have of the ground, the person, and the helping resources of the pastor, there are several ingredients in designing a strategy for pastoral care to those suffering loss.

Be informed. There are two areas in which we need to gather information. The first is *knowledge.* Familiarity with the theological and clinical perspectives on grief help us to be more observant and more competent in carrying out our ministry. Regular reading about grief helps us to remain alert. Since grief and loss or fear of loss are the most common times we are called, this is a major area needing our attention.

We also must keep informed about *what losses are occurring* in the places we serve. Sometimes we hear about a death first from the funeral home. Encourage the members of the congregation to call when a death occurs; it is better to get several calls than none. We can keep informed if we cultivate a good grapevine. Publishing lists of losses for which we want to be called keeps the community alert. The laying off of employees by companies generates losses that call for our attention. Reading the obituaries often reveals deaths of relatives of our parishioners, and making a visit is very much in order.

Remember too that the grief doesn't end after the first few weeks. The visits we make during the stage of remembering are often crucial in the adjustment to loss.

Be present with the persons who have suffered loss. Visits at first may be brief. What we say is not nearly so important as whether we were there. That is what is remembered most. Longer visits are more in order during the later stages of grief, and we must *plan* those visits so that more immediate issues don't allow us to forget. In our being present, it is important not to push people to move on through the process unless there is clear evidence of being stuck and there is agreement in the appropriate community that this is so. We exercise our initiative and our faithfulness in times of grief by being willing to deal with people's concerns, not pushing them to "get over it."

Be willing to leave. People need our presence and our reassurance, but they also need times to themselves. Too much hovering may communicate to them that we don't think they will make it. Our absences may teach them as much as our presence. We are coming to share with them, not to take over for them.

Be alert to special needs. Familiarity with the stages of grief helps us to plan our visits. We know, for instance, that in the first stages presence is more important than talking. In later stages, it is important to allow and encourage the grieved person to talk about what has happened and what he or she remembers. As Lindemann observed, "comfort alone does not provide adequate assistance." Pain must be acknowledged rather than avoided. Fears must be talked about rather than repressed. Plans must be made rather than getting someone else to take over for the person. The sorrow needs to be expressed rather than simply acknowledged. All these needs are part of the normal grief process, and they must be spoken to some degree by the grieved person.

Remember that they may be spoken to someone other than us. We often assume that we must hear them if they are to "count." But if we have not heard them, a gentle inquiry or expression of hope that "you have someone whom you can tell about all your thoughts and feelings" helps to ascertain that it is taking place. Or such a suggestion may start the process.

Watch for signs of the process becoming abnormal. If you

see any, consult with others who know the person or know the grief process well.

Be mindful of the various resources that may be helpful to the person. We have mentioned passages of Scripture. Prayer with the person is often desired but is not mentioned out of fear that we may resent requests. Willingness to hear expressions of guilt is often important. Reading about grief is often helpful during private moments. Encouragement of expression of grief and thanksgiving through prayer is frequently of help. One characteristic of grief is that normal resources are often forgotten, and reminders are helpful. Suggestions about visiting friends or having them in for visits help the process of reinvestment to begin when appropriate. Making suggestions to friends about including the bereaved in activities after a time is helpful to the community in making its continuing response.

REFLECTION

Remember some of the losses you have experienced during your life. List them. Look at the variety of events, and let yourself become aware that most of us are in several processes of grief at any given time. Select a particular loss in your life and remember the responses from others that were most helpful to you. Remember, too, some of the things you wished for and did not receive during that experience.

Select some reading about grief to aid you in becoming more familiar with its nature. Try first to apply the understanding to yourself. Then begin to plan some ways you will attempt to take initiative and be faithful to persons experiencing grief and loss.

For Further Reading

Bowers, Margaretta K., et al. *Counseling the Dying.* Thomas Nelson & Sons, 1964.

Freese, Arthur S. *Help for Your Grief.* Schocken Books, 1977.

Grollman, Earl. *Living—When a Loved One Has Died.* Beacon Press, 1977.

Grollman, Earl, ed. *Explaining Death to Children.* Beacon Press, 1967.

Jackson, Edgar. *Telling a Child About Death.* Channel Press, 1965.

Jewett, John. *After Suicide.* Christian Care Book. Westminster Press, 1980.

Kübler-Ross, Elisabeth. *On Death and Dying.* Macmillan Co., 1969.

Lewis, C. S. *A Grief Observed.* Seabury Press, 1963.

Lindemann, Erich, and Lindemann, Elizabeth. *Beyond Grief: Studies in Crisis Intervention.* Jason Aronson, 1979.

Menninger, Karl. *Man Against Himself.* Harcourt, Brace and Co., 1938.

Oates, Wayne E. *Pastoral Care and Counseling in Grief and Separation.* Fortress Press, 1976.

Pretzel, Paul W. *Understanding and Counseling the Suicidal Person.* Abingdon Press, 1972.

Reeves, Robert B., ed. *Pastoral Care of the Dying and the Bereaved.* Health Sciences Publishing Corp., 1973.

Schoenberg, Bernard, ed. *Bereavement: Its Psychosocial Aspects.* Columbia University Press, 1975.

———. *Loss and Grief: Psychological Management in Medical Practice.* Columbia University Press, 1970.

Soulen, Richard N., ed. *Care for the Dying.* John Knox Press, 1975.

Switzer, David K. *The Dynamics of Grief.* Abingdon Press, 1970.

Tatelbaum, Judy. *The Courage to Grieve.* Lippincott & Crowell, 1980.

12

A Pastoral Approach
to Illness

Illness is an experience in which our theology and the traditional resources of pastoral care converge in a most dramatic light. In illness we see that we are whole persons rather than beings who can neatly be diagnosed as having physical *or* emotional problems. In our encouragement to people to call the minister in times of illness, we suddenly discover the number of people who do not want to *admit* illness to anyone. Illness, then, is an experience in which we have much opportunity to exercise initiative and faithfulness.

Many pastors dread the "hospital call" because they feel themselves to be in foreign territory. The hospital somehow belongs to the medical people, and the temptation is to stay away or act as though you are a medical person, too. Often we are notified of illness by the hospital rather than by the parishioner, and we are exercising initiative when not first invited by the patient. In this chapter we will discuss the various signs of illness to which the pastor should be attuned. Further, we will speak of various caring approaches, depending on the nature of the illness and the motivation exhibited.

EARLY DIAGNOSIS OR "IT SHOULDN'T BE SO"

Theological Backdrop

When we discuss illness, we are speaking of an undesirable state for human beings. Thus, it is important to remind ourselves of some of the theological characteristics we have claimed as "natural" for human beings.

First, we are *limited* creatures. We are not always able to know we are sick. It is possible for us to function in quite normal fashion while some illness is making its initial attack or even advancing to a critical stage. Cancer and heart disease are probably the most commonly known examples of such an occurrence. To greater or lesser degrees many people feel anxious about the possibility of carrying around some as yet undiagnosed disease that will spell great difficulty for them. Our limitation may be the inability to perceive something quite observable to others. How often has someone pointed out that we look "white as a sheet" or "flushed"? Later, we discovered that we had a temperature, or we came down with some illness. People can note that we seem more "nervous than usual" when it had not occurred to us that we were strung out from hard work or emotional pressures. Or our manner of relating to family and friends gradually changes, and we are late in recognizing it. A person under stress may develop backaches, chest pains, or gastrointestinal difficulties. The physical expression is a first acknowledgment of an ongoing emotional burden. Often this is the case with persons who have denied their grief for years, unaware how the loss has ravaged them. Finally, during an illness, they become aware of the pain that has stayed just out of sight over the years.

Many times our limitations combine forces with the second characteristic: our *gifts*. Perceiving difficulty we do not want to acknowledge, we skillfully use our gifts to cover up a problem. "Out of sight, out of mind" becomes the motto. Persons with ability to work hard or to prosper can use those "gifts" to "cover up" difficulties. Alcoholics with money can remain hidden behind polished doors and be cared for by hired help, never having to acknowledge the problem and confront the need for change. The person with serious problems in a marital relationship can be a productive worker, drawing praise for monumental accomplishments, all the time using that energy to disguise the fact that things at home are miserable.

And third, we are *sinful* creatures who will distort the reality of our limitations or our gifts. We may know that we are ill, know that we are skillfully disguising it, and convince ourselves that it is "the best thing to do" for all concerned. We can convince ourselves and others that things are much better, or much worse, than is actually the case. So much is invested in preserving a certain image of who we are. When something like illness appears, shaking up that image, we can take in all the information and then convince ourselves that it is all a mistake. Ignore it, and it will go away.

Those theological characteristics remind us of what we may be up against in attempting to care for ourselves and others. People do not readily admit to illness. Even ministers "won't be sick" because they have to take care of others. Right?

Cultivating the Tools of Observation

We must develop skills for coping with characteristics that tend to be damaging to ourselves and those for whom we care. If we know that we cannot always depend on people to tell us when things are going poorly, there are other signals for which we must watch.

One of those things to watch is *behavior*. People tend to

be creatures of habit. When behavior changes, something else is going on. Of course, something good may be happening rather than something bad. But in any case, we must train ourselves to look for changes in behavior.

Most helping professionals watch five major areas for change: eating, sleeping, family life, recreational activities, and working performance satisfaction. If changes begin to occur in several of those areas, then some inquiry needs to be made. For instance, if a person suddenly eats much less than usual, sleeps more than usual, stops a regular form of exercise, and becomes undependable at work, something is happening. It may be a temporary crisis, an attack of the flu, or a stressful preoccupation. Listen and watch for those kinds of changes.

It is also important to listen. Clues may appear in friendly conversation. The person who begins to say regularly, "I am working so hard that I'm killing myself at a young age," may be doing more than casual complaining. There may be some important things happening in his or her life. That comment may have been "dropped" in an attempt to gauge your sensitivity and dependability in following up.

Curiosity as an Expression of Pastoral Care

Once we have made the observation, heard the comment, and become reasonably convinced that our theological affirmations are visible in this concrete human experience, we are faced with what to do! It is time to "make an intervention." We may jump the gun and be embarrassed, or we may expose an area in need of attention and hasten the process of cure or help.

One major expression of pastoral care is curiosity or interest. At a discreet time and place, through a visit, phone call, or letter, let a person know that you have noticed and you care. We may be accused of being nosy or get surprise and gratitude for being able to talk, since you "happened to mention it." The following is an example of curiosity used pastorally:

> **PASTOR:** Betty, I am glad to catch you here in the hallway. I've been meaning to say something to you.
> **BETTY:** Oh, what is that?
> **P:** Well, I've noticed you looking awfully fatigued over the last few weeks. And I've worried about you.
> **B:** What do you mean? (She looks distressed.) What have you noticed?
> **P:** Well, at the session meeting two weeks ago you looked preoccupied and not as alert as you usually are. Then, when you've dropped your children off at kindergarten, you haven't bounced through and visited with us in the office as you so often do. And, I don't know, you've just looked worried.
> **B:** Well, I didn't know it was showing. I mean . . . well, I found a lump in my breast about three weeks ago, and I have been putting off going to the doctor about it. But putting it off isn't helping any. My husband says I'm grouchy lately. Now you are noticing changes in me. Maybe I should go ahead and get this thing checked. Keeping it to myself isn't helping anybody.
> **P:** Well, if it'll get you to check out something like that, I'm glad I said something. Will you let me know when you are going and how it turns out?

Of course, the success stories are the ones I most like to tell, but not all problems turn out that way. Nonetheless, when a few turn out the way this one did, it makes all the others worth the effort.

Direct Intervention as an Expression of Pastoral Care

Sometimes expression of curiosity is not enough or even adequate. Such was the case when I was called by the neighbor of a parishioner. For several days she had not seen this gentleman, who lived alone. Worried, she did not know him well enough to go into his house but wanted someone to. I went, knocked on the door, got no response, checked with other people who knew him, and discovered concern among them for his welfare. Returning to the house, I looked in the windows and saw him in bed. After I had pounded on the window for some time, he slowly stood up and came to the door.

> **PASTOR:** Hello, Mr. G. Several folks have been worried about you, and I came by to see how you are doing.
> **MR. G:** Go away. Can't you see I'm sick?
> **P:** I'm sorry about that. Can I help you in some way?
> **G:** No, I want to die. Don't bother me. Don't interfere. I'm an old man, and I want to die. Go away.
> **P:** I'd like to come in for a while and talk with you.
> **G:** Suit yourself. (He turns, walks back to his bedroom, and falls onto the bed.)
> **P:** Mr. G., have you had anything to eat?
> **G:** (He doesn't reply. I look around the house. The refrigerator is absolutely empty, nothing to eat or drink. Garbage in the can smells several days old.)
> **P:** Mr. G., I am going to call a doctor.
> **G:** Go away; don't interfere. Nobody can help me. I want to die.

After several exchanges like that, I got in touch with some family and friends, and we forcefully had him hospitalized, where he was treated for malnutrition, and an anemia problem was diagnosed. Now he continues to live by himself with reasonable comfort, and still gruffly notifies me that I shouldn't have "trespassed" that day I came to see him. However, there is a twinkle in his eye when he says it. He also continues to see a counselor once a month where he talks of the grief over the death of his wife and the adjustment to living alone.

Summary

Knowledge of human nature, combined with awareness of the importance of being sensitive, gives us authority to exercise initiative in the lives of persons who are in need of help but have not yet seen or agreed that help is needed. Of course, we must also be prepared to make a proper referral if it is needed. Many persons already know from whom they will get help once they decide to ask for it.

THE ACUTE TIME OF ILLNESS

Once diagnosis has been made and help has been requested, a person is in the acute stage of treatment for illness. Trust in the treatment is being established. Much pain and discomfort may be taking place emotionally and physically. It may be a time of psychiatric, medical, or surgical hospitalization. The role of the pastor now shifts. Primary responsibility for the patient is in the hands of another helping professional. However, the pastor continues to exercise faithfulness in a variety of ways.

Theological Backdrop

As before, reminders of our theological understanding of human nature stand out during the acute phase of an illness. First, limitations are clearly visible! Anxiety, pain, slow recovery, limitations in relating effectively to other people— all these are graphically experienced by the person as patient. Gifts can be geared to swift and knowledgeable recovery, or distortions can lead to a denial of whatever gifts are available. The relational and responsive dimensions of human nature are very evident in *having* to depend on other people, often in embarrassing ways. And the developmental character of human beings is reinforced by the reality of having to let nature take its course and deciding whether to be cooperative with it. Often, during the acute phase of an illness, these issues become conscious with people in a way that has not occurred before. It is an occasion that can lead a person to reflect on self, relationships, hopes, and plans for the future.

Regular Visitation

Visits are primarily symbolic during an acute stage of treatment. For a pastor to consume large amounts of time and emotional investment with a patient often may interfere with the treatment process. Assurance of care is communicated by a brief visit. The promise to return and inquiries that allow the patient to tell only what he or she wants to tell are important. Willingness to listen is a major contribution, especially if the care is being rendered in a medical-surgical hospital. Few staff are there with the time or responsibility to listen. In a psychiatric hospital, time to listen is a part of the treatment plan. Whenever you question the helpfulness or propriety of your visits, inquire of hospital staff. Let them know who you are and the nature of your interest. You will then be regarded as a member of the team, rather than as an interference.

Seldom are persons able or willing to engage in deep reflection during the acute phase because of pain, discomfort, fear, or distractions. But frequently there are expressions of a desire to do so. The pastor can be sensitive to those expressions, provide openings for them in conversation, and provide assurance that such issues will not be forgotten.

Many people, in a state of panic over their condition, try to make major decisions or sweeping promises. Listening to such exclamations is important. Rarely, however, does it make sense to attempt to "argue" persons out of their fear. Sometimes, however, decisions *do* have to be made, wills written, etc. Sensitivity and interdisciplinary cooperation are very important when such circumstances arise.

Remembering the Family

Because of the dramatic nature and surprise accompanying an acute phase of illness, families often are ignored while attention is focused on the patient. They are consulted about treatment for the patient and then left alone while the process is carried out. Frequently it is difficult for them to obtain information about their family member or close friend, as if the reports were "secret possessions" of the people who "really understand."

Major ministry is rendered by the pastor who spends time with the family during this acute period. Fears for the patient, frustration with treatment process, their quandary about decisions to make and other sources of anxiety need to be spoken. Often we will have knowledge about some procedures and can serve as a guide through some of the technicalities. Our contact with other helping professions can be of help to a family as we make contacts for them, obtain information, and serve as an "interpreter" of language that is difficult for them to understand. Of course, many times they can understand very well, but the shock suppresses their comprehension, and they need to hear again. If we have been with them when they first hear news, we can repeat it to them when they are able to listen more attentively.

Praying with the family, sitting with them, helping the rest of the supportive community get into action, and making regular contact are crucial expressions of the initiative and faithfulness we have mentioned so often.

Small children and adolescents too often are neglected during this period. Left with baby-sitters or told to get their own meals, they both fear what is happening and are angry at being left out as if they "didn't care or know" what is going on. Private visits, even for a very few minutes, give children assurance that their thoughts and feelings matter, too. Reminding adults of the importance of including the children is also important.

Interdisciplinary Cooperation

If there is confusion in understanding, anger about treatment information, or if major decisions are being made, it is important to confer and exchange information with the other members of the treatment team. Relay of messages through a secretary, quick visits in the halls of the hospital, or exchange of letters are helpful avenues for making contact if more lengthy conversations do not seem necessary. Remember to identify yourself and your relationship with the patient and/or family for the sake of confidentiality issues that may arise in discussing the situation.

THE CONVALESCENT PERIOD OF ILLNESS

Following the acute phase of an illness there is often a longer recuperative phase. The patient may continue to stay in a hospital for part of this before returning home. With the absence of the intensity of treatment and the maintenance of what come to be routine methods of care, the role of the minister continues to be important.

Theological Backdrop

Characteristics discussed under the prediagnosis phase may return. Persons may begin to act as if they had not been sick. A coronary patient exerts himself or herself too much.

Persons ordered not to get up begin to assert their independence by getting out of bed without assistance. Psychiatric patients may begin to subject themselves to emotional pressures they are not yet ready to handle. Limits are again being denied, gifts at concealment are reactivated, distortions of the real picture begin to recur, need for others and the process of recovery are ignored.

Of course, this is not always the case. Desire to reflect on what has been learned through the experience may result in profound new awareness of limits, gifts, distortions, etc. Whatever the case, the minister has an opportunity to keep tabs on what is happening with patient and family—an opportunity not ordinarily available to the other helping professions.

Regular Visitation

As with the earlier phases, the importance of visitation continues. Perhaps this is the most important time of all. Too frequently the patient and family are forgotten after the acute phase. It is assumed that things are back to normal, and people return to their own routines or rush off to the next crisis. Patient and family can be left with a feeling of being deserted and left alone to cope with the consequences of the illness.

Visits with patient and family, sometimes together and sometimes separately, can be very redemptive. Decisions about "where to from here?" may need to be made. The pastor can listen, serve as a sounding board, and provide avenues for further reflection.

The nature of such visits can vary from quite informal to quite formal. Dropping by, much as a friend would do, is often the most comfortable procedure for all concerned. On the other hand, if a person has identified very specific areas for attention, the making of regular appointments may best symbolize the seriousness devoted to the enterprise. Visits in the home reveal a great deal about the adjustment and recovery process. Notable changes in dress, care of the home, presence or absence of certain family members all can give subtle clues about how things are going. Frequently these clues would not appear in an office visit. Also, people may raise concerns in a relaxed visit in their home that they would be uncomfortable raising in a more formal trip to an office.

Remember that these visits are for patient and family, including the children. The adjustment process during the convalescent period shapes family patterns and affects the "system" in many ways. We have the opportunity to be a part of that shaping process if we exercise the initiative in a faithful way.

Special Resources

Reference has been made to dropping by "much as a friend." More should take place than passing the time of day. In a casual yet concerned manner, the pastor can inquire about the way the convalescence is going, concerns the person may have, feelings of hope, discouragement, etc. Such inquiries are usually best made in the form of invitations to talk about these matters rather than demands to discuss them. The authority of the minister tends to make it "okay" to let down some of the "cover" and talk because "that is what you talk to a minister about." Patients often have been discouraged from talking about serious matters. Their visitors only want to hear encouragement, not discouragement. Such a game shouldn't have to be played with the pastor.

Time is often available for reading, and suggestions of Scripture, devotions, self-understanding approaches are welcomed. A good pastoral library is a worthwhile investment, placing carefully chosen books in the hands of recovering persons *with the promise to talk about their reactions.*

Many convalescents are reflecting on and struggling with desires to evaluate, change, and/or repent of past patterns of living. They may be uncomfortable in first mentioning such concerns. Openness demonstrated by the pastor for listening to "anything" sets the tone in a way that may enable them to initiate such a conversation. Expressions of hope often need to be voiced, but there is fear in saying them out loud. Again, they need to know that there is a ready and understanding ear to hear them.

Maintenance of Interprofessional Contacts

While in most circumstances there is no necessity for continued contact with physician or other primary health professional, observations may be gained in your visits that would be helpful to them. Phone calls, letters, or requests for a meeting are quite appropriate and often valued.

SPECIAL AREAS OF CONCERN

Diagnosis

Because of the general nature of this chapter, specific references have not been made to particular *types* of physical and/or emotional illness. The stages that have been discussed are characteristic of them all, and the general principles of pastoral care would hold.

However, it is important for any pastor to develop knowledge of the variety of diagnostic labels that are used to describe illnesses. Familiarity with the effects of cancer, heart disease, and various surgical procedures provides valuable information about what to anticipate as an "expected" response to the procedure. Familiarity with commonly used drugs aids in understanding the manner in which people respond to us and the dramatic differences in response from one visit to the next. In mental and emotional disorders, which evidence themselves primarily in behavior and styles of relating, it is essential to understand what is known about these different disorders and to be aware of the current understanding of causes and treatment.

Therefore, it is important for a pastor to familiarize herself or himself with current literature. Maintain contact with persons in various specialties in the helping community. Several such persons in your local parish can serve as a valuable resource committee. These people become, as it were, "consultants" for your own continuing education and caring. A book such as the *Diagnostic and Statistical Manual of Mental Disorders* provides helpful and concrete indications of the various problems in the emotional/psychiatric field. A good medical dictionary is an important resource.

Confidentiality

References have been made throughout this chapter to communication with family, patient, and health care professionals. Often the question arises, "What should I tell or not tell when these matters have been discussed in privacy?" The answer is not easy, but there are some general rules of thumb that prove helpful.

First, confidentiality is designed to be *helpful* to the patient and family, and to prevent harm, although it may not prevent discomfort. The rules of confidentiality mean, then, that we discuss material *if* its aim is to benefit the patient. Then we talk only with people who are *equipped, trained,* and *trustworthy* for the care of this particular person.

Second, confidentiality is a concept that works within a *team orientation.* Health care is too complex to be practiced by one person. It is practiced by a combination of skilled people with varied training and interests. Information gained by one is often of help to all. Confidentiality is confined to those persons involved in the treatment.

Third, confidentiality sounds like a secretive word, but it

calls for real *openness.* It is important *not* to promise a patient that you will keep secrets. Instead, my promise is that I will not discuss material with anyone other than people involved in the care of that person. Obviously, any decision on my part to discuss it with someone else will be made known to the patient. Part of a person's willingness to engage you in a confidential relationship must be based on confidence that *you* will make responsible decisions, not that person's right to make your decisions for you!

Fourth, confidentiality calls for a skilled *manner* of sharing information. If a physician has bad news for a patient or family and tells you about it, an important part of that conversation should be *how* and *when* that information will be shared. The team concept is very clear here. Once you have gained the information, dashing off to tell the family would be irresponsible in terms of confidentiality. Decisions must be made together to arrive at the most helpful and least harmful manner of delivering the news.

In essence, confidentiality carries the meaning of *caring.* Information is important enough to be handled with care. Therefore, we call it confidential.

REFLECTION

Care of persons during illness calls for sensitivity and knowledge. It is all too easy to drop by without a clear understanding of the effects of illness on patient, family, and community. Structure some time in the near future to learn about the health care fields, especially those which can educate you further about the varied expressions of illness. Pay close attention to the interrelationships of the physical and emotional.

Take some time, too, to reflect on your own response to illness, and that of people who are important to you. Learn from yourself about what you need, what you expect. Find out how similar or dissimilar other people are in their reactions and expectations.

For Further Reading

American Psychiatric Association. *Diagnostic and Statistical Manual of Mental Disorders.* 3d ed. American Psychiatric Association, 1980.

Bennett, George. *When the Mental Patient Comes Home.* Christian Care Book. Westminster Press, 1980.

Cabot, Richard, and Dicks, Russell L. *The Art of Ministering to the Sick.* Macmillan Co., 1936.

Cox-Gedmark, Jan. *Coping with Physical Disability.* Christian Care Book. Westminster Press, 1980.

Draper, Edgar. *Psychiatry and Pastoral Care.* Prentice-Hall, 1965.

Faber, Heije. *Pastoral Care in the Modern Hospital.* Westminster Press, 1972.

Fairchild, Roy W. *Finding Hope Again: A Pastor's Guide to Counseling Depressed Persons.* Harper & Row, 1980.

Fieve, Ronald R. *Moodswing: The Third Revolution in Psychiatry.* William Morrow & Co., 1975.

Grollman, Earl. *When Your Loved One Is Dying.* Beacon Press, 1980.

Menninger, Karl. *The Vital Balance.* Viking Press, 1963.

Oates, Wayne E. *The Religious Care of the Psychiatric Patient.* Westminster Press, 1978.

Schmidt, Paul F. *Coping with Difficult People.* Christian Care Book. Westminster Press, 1980.

Shapero, Lucy, and Goodman, Anthony A. *Never Say Die: A Doctor and Patient Talk About Breast Cancer.* Appleton-Century-Crofts, 1980.

Turnage, Mac and Anne. *More Than You Dare to Ask: The First Year of Living with Cancer.* John Knox Press, 1976.

13
A Pastoral Approach
to Family and Marriage

Family and marriage issues are major components of the life of the church. Marriages traditionally are performed in the church, or at least by a minister. Indeed the church frequently refers to itself as the "family" of God. Many pastoral opportunities exist for creative care of family and marriage members, including those who are single members of the church family.

All too often in the history of the church, nurture has been provided for those about to be married or for those no longer married, but seldom until recent years has specific nurture been encouraged for persons *while* married. Also, the tendency of the church to place such importance on family and marriage life has seemed to isolate those who are unmarried, leaving many with a sense of being second-class citizens.

BIBLICAL AND THEOLOGICAL RESOURCES

In order to minister and be sensitive to the dynamics of families and marriages, we must have some commitment to and understanding of the theological nature and intention of marriage and family. Among the richest places to look for such understanding are the first two chapters of the book of

Genesis and the theological interpretations made of those creation narratives.

A Community for Nurturing Children

The marital relationship is a microcosm of the community of faith, and provides the nurture crucial for healthy human growth. Marriage, then, is the focal center for family life and the rearing of children. It is the context within which one learns about the meaning of faithfulness to one another, the experience of forgiveness when one person wrongs another, and the acknowledgment of commonality. The family, and all of us have one, provides the context within which we learn what it is to be a member of the community of humankind.

Characteristics of the Partnership

The intended relationship between wife and husband is found in Gen. 2:18: "Then the Lord God said, 'It is not good that the man should be alone; I will make him a helper fit for him.' " While chauvinistic interpretations have been made of that verse, they miss the signal meaning of the Hebrew word translated in the RSV as "fit."

Three dimensions fill out the meaning of that concept. First is the dimension of *equality.* For the woman to be "fit" for the man, or for the man and the woman to be "fit" for each other, there must be equal regard in terms of status and worth. The relationship intended in this creation narrative is one in which each is "worthy" of the other. Some may be quick to cite the numerous examples of women being treated as chattel property throughout the Old and New Testaments. Nonetheless, the *intention* is clearly present in the initial declaration. These two persons are to be held in mutual honor. Their status is the same.

A second dimension of *adequacy* is also important. Adequacy carries the meaning of being "capable of responding." Each partner has the capacity to respond to the other, to work to meet the needs each experiences and declares to each other. Combined with the dimension of equality, the adequacy of the partners means that they are equipped to respond and work in partnership with each other in a way that no other creature can understand. Both are limited, mind you. That is one of our earlier affirmations about human nature. Their adequacy, then, becomes a necessity. They need each other to live more fully, and they are adequate to work out cooperative means for doing so.

A third dimension is involved in the "fitness" of the relationship between husband and wife: *differentness*. The two are equal to, adequate for, and different from each other. These differences are not in terms of status or capacity, but of an order difficult to identify in specific ways. Perhaps the differences are ones of experience, perception, and response. Perhaps they are not mutually exclusive differences that could neatly be assigned to one sex or the other. Nonetheless, the differences are of such a degree that the two will never fully understand each other.

Those dimensions involved in the Hebrew concept of "fitness" are useful to us in understanding the nature of the relationship intended in the partnership created by God. It is a partnership that is incredible in its potential for creative living or destructive conflict. As the characteristics are denied, so isolation and deterioration are promoted. As those characteristics are acknowledged, opportunities for richly living out the intention arise.

Along with those dimensions which comprise the manner in which two partners should view each other must be considered the concept of *faithfulness*. Marriage is intended to be a relationship in which two partners are permanently faithful to each other. The theological importance of faithfulness is demonstrated in Scripture by regular usage of marriage as a paradigm for God's faithfulness to us. In those moments in which we are faithful, forgiving one another, we experience something of the reality of God's faithfulness to us.

In seeking to understand the importance of faithfulness, we must also discuss brokenness. Marriages do end. Our limitations and our sinfulness contribute to many tragic ends for such hopeful beginnings. It is interesting that we learn much of Jesus' stress on the permanence of marriage in his response to a question about divorce. Divorce is one of the manifestations of limitedness and sin that are part of human nature. When two people divorce, they have fallen short of God's *intention* for marriage. In spite of that falling short, however, God forgives. That does not do away with accountability or the pain of the brokenness, but God's faithfulness is greater than our capacity to be faithful. Thus, while divorce is to be regarded with sadness and disappointment, and often anger, there is reassurance in God's forgiveness that one's gifts are still intact, as well as one's limits. Something can be learned. The community of faith is still called to be faithful to divorced persons, as it is called to be faithful to all of its members, who are also sinners.

PSYCHOLOGICAL RESOURCES

With concepts in mind about the nature and intention of families and marriages, we now turn to the research and perspectives of the social sciences to aid us in identifying clinical indicators of health and deterioration in familial and marital lives.

A Perspective on Conflict

Perspective on conflict is based on an assumption about health in relationships: differences that exist between individuals in a healthy relationship should be aired and dealt with rather than repressed or ignored. Differences (as indicated in our biblical study) are viewed as healthy and natural. They are a source for much strong feeling between partners. The absence of acknowledged differences and strong feelings may indicate an absence of emotional investment in the relationship.

When differences are handled openly, partners have the opportunity to deal with them in a manner which has the health of the relationship as its aim. Issues can be faced and adjustments made, and the faithfulness carries them through.

A Developmental Perspective

When differences are dealt with in a manner that aims to win no matter what it takes, major problems arise. *Assaults,* or *attacks* (verbal or physical), are a first warning signal. For example, two partners may be concerned about bad grades made by their child at school. A healthy conversation would reveal differences of opinion about helping the child: television or no television; punishment or encouragement. The strategies would be debated, and a trial plan agreed upon. If the relationship has deteriorated into attacks, the child's welfare disappears as the topic of concern. Accusations consume energy and feelings run high. This warning signal may be, at the same time, an indication that there is hope. Some writers, such as George Bach, maintain that conflict is a very hopeful sign, and he encourages people to learn how to fight fairly. Differences then become productive stimuli for the relationship rather than destructive ones.

A second warning signal frequently appears if a relationship worsens: *withdrawal.* The attacks and the pain of winning or losing become too much for one or both partners. A retreat is sounded, or more often it is not sounded but simply carried out. Husband or wife finds commitments that keep him or her away from home or at least away from each other. Television, reading, working in the basement, or

spending more time with the kids become calculated efforts
not to communicate with each other. Feelings may intensify.
Imagination about what the other partner is thinking or
doing may become exaggerated. There is also an unspoken
agreement "not to let anyone else know how unhappy we
are with each other." Depression or high irritability is often
characteristic of this stage.

A further step toward deterioration may occur with the
involvement of a third party. Telling a child or other extended
family member, telling a close friend or a business associate,
having an affair, or seeking professional help are only a few
of the alternatives. Immersing oneself in work or becoming
very dedicated to a cause can be a third-party involvement.
It is the finding of someone or something else to invest
oneself in. The choice of a third party immensely affects
whether the relationship will seek to rebuild or terminate.
Now someone else knows! There is relief, as well as embarrassment, at that point. Now decisions and action can be
worked out without quite as much defensiveness. Often the
minister is the third-party choice made by one or both partners.

If the third-party involvement does not lead to repair of
the relationship, the fourth stage of deterioration is one of
intensified attacks and formal threats about ending the relationship. Consultation with lawyers, trial separations, threats to
sue for child custody, public ridicule, and financial irrespon-
sibility all are indications that this fourth stage is in full
force. Sadly enough, as with all the earlier stages, people
may "choose" to remain in this stage for long periods of
time.

A fifth stage is one of *formally ending the relationship.* In the
case of marriage, this stage is a legal one. Depending on the
laws involved and the willingness of the partners to go
through with it, the process can be relatively short or ex-
ceedingly long. Many people use the legal phase to further

embarrass or attack each other. In states where no-fault divorce has been instituted, a partner may choose to get the court to grant custody of the children, declaring the other parent "unfit." On the other hand, many couples come to this phase with conviction that the decision is right for them and seek to avoid any more harm to children and each other than is unavoidable.

A final stage then occurs: *grief.* While surprising at first, it should not be. Even if the decision is viewed as right and best, there is still grief at the loss of all the hopes for what that relationship was intended to be. Too often people expect the divorced persons to be happy, when such is not the case. Wounds must heal, self-confidence must be restored, a new support community must be established. Much of what was said in Chapter 11 on grief is applicable here.

While the examples in describing the process have focused on marital partners, the stages of deterioration can also be applied to relationships between friends, parents and children, siblings, and to a variety of other bonds between human beings. The value of knowing such signals is that we may catch ourselves early and seek reconciliation. In like manner, we may see the signals in others and express our concern in the hope that they can do early preventative maintenance instead of waiting longer and making restoration more difficult.

The Family as a System

Another view of family has emerged in recent years that is of help. The family is seen as a *system.* Dating back at least to the advent of child psychiatry, this concept is based on the discovery that disturbed children could often be removed from homes, treated, and restored to normal functioning. However, when returned to their homes, they became disturbed again. Conclusion? The family itself was disturbed, and the child was the symptom, or "identified patient," of that larger disturbance. To know that someone is a family therapist does not tell us much about what will be done in therapy, but it does tell us that there is a "belief system" which asserts, first, that a disturbed individual is merely the symptom or warning signal of a family or group that is in distress. A troubled individual is the visible manifestation of a more far-reaching disturbance. Therefore, when a family requests help for one person, the only effective treatment is one that works with the entire family.

A second belief underlying the work of family therapists is that an emotional disturbance has deep roots over several generations. Some individuals marry and do not have the perspective or the training to adapt and solve problems that emerge in their relationship. They live as if they were still in their family of origin. Then they learn to live in a way that does not deal effectively with present problems. A system is developed that is unhealthy and unrealistic.

The third belief of most family therapists is that this system must be interrupted in a manner that does not allow it to continue in its former manner. The form of the interruption is where the varying techniques appear. Some therapists will interrupt in a forceful, confronting way. Others will invite the family into a calm, analytical examination of what is going on. Others will model a more healthy form of communication and invite the family to imitate the model and then make adjustments to it that will use their own unique gifts and make allowances for their limits.

The value of such a view is manifold. There is acknowledgment of the communicative or responsive characteristic of human nature. We do not grow and change in isolation, and we cannot do so in a way that does not affect other people. Furthermore, the limitations of our growth will come to haunt us in the present if we do not live in a context that encourages us to grow and change. The view of family as system is quite compatible with our theological assumptions about human nature. Some forms of family therapy will not take the limits sufficiently into account, but there is much clinical research in this field that is helpful to us in finding concrete ways to express our theological convictions in pastoral care.

AN INCIDENT OF FAMILY DISTURBANCE

Ted and Alice came from similar family backgrounds, reasonably affluent and warm in nature. Both had dated extensively in high school and college before meeting in their last year of college. After two years of dating and establishment in jobs, they decided to marry. By all appearances they were quite compatible in terms of interests and choice of friends. Wanting to establish themselves on a solid and independent financial base, they waited to have a child until they had been married five years. Both looked forward to the child eagerly, and for the first two years in the life of their daughter they seemed quite happy.

They came to their pastor during the child's third year and reported that they were quite unhappy with each other. As the child had become more and more verbal (and able to play the two parents off against each other) they had found themselves involved in increasingly vicious arguments about the handling of responsibilities. Who was going to take care of the child when? Who decided about disciplinary actions? Each was accusing the other of choosing up sides with the child against the other partner. In short, they had not been able to handle a third member of the family. Their ability to understand each other without talking had broken down when their child began to test them.

After some careful and determined work on understanding each other better, getting some time away from the child for each other, and agreeing to sit down regularly to talk about themselves and their family system, their commitment to each other seemed renewed.

A PASTORAL STRATEGY

Dealing pastorally with couples like Ted and Alice calls for both immediate kinds of intervention and reflection on preventive maintenance to identify other couples and families before they come to such a point.

Educational Programs on Family Life

One of the ways in which the principle of initiative can be exercised in the lives of families is to design varying kinds of educational formats to educate people on the stages of development and the warning signals of deterioration. Regular programs of this sort, as well as attention in preaching, often give people "permission" to identify themselves as in need of help.

It is important to remember in designing such programs that people vary in terms of their limits and gifts and thus in terms of the kind of program to which they will be responsive. Some will come, for instance, for discussion and sharing. Others will avoid any situation in which they might have to say anything. The word "group" will attract some and turn away others. The word "class" will do the same. Choice of descriptive terminology will shape the makeup of any program format, and varying the terminology and format makes the opportunity available to far more people.

Much of the developmental information already discussed in this chapter and earlier ones is of interest to people. Phone calls for help often result from being informed about the warning signals. The teaching dimension of pastoral care is of extreme value in ministry to families and marriages.

Premarital Counseling

With many persons, the only personal contact with the minister is when they marry. The premarital conversations provide important opportunities for education and expression of care. While many ministers are pessimistic about the effect that premarital counseling will have, at the very least it provides an occasion to establish rapport. That rapport may be what enables a couple to ask for help later if problems develop.

In premarital counseling, questions and information about the warning signals help them to become aware of things to watch for in their relationship. A careful pastor may discover that some of the signals are already present and may initiate several conversations before even consenting to perform the wedding. While it is true that the least opportune time to provide premarital education is after two persons have already decided to marry, better that time than never! A good deal of literature with suggested formats is available on premarital counseling. Or you may prefer to design your own.

Premarital counseling really is best done earlier in life, before a life's partner has been chosen. Try, as a part of the educational programs suggested above, to set up regular "premarital" discussions with children and youth in the church. Education on communication patterns, the effect of differing values on relationships, and the stages through which families and marriages go will be of great interest to them.

Marital Growth Groups

Following an educational presentation, many couples, or even families, enjoy meeting regularly to discuss the health of their relationships. This may be done in terms of quite personal sharing, or in a more general way with discussions of new books read or new ideas for promoting health in families. Often such groups will meet for years. Much literature is available on formats and other suggestions for the ongoing process of such gatherings.

Visits on "Rumor"

One of the difficulties in ministry is knowing what to do with all the rumors that come to the pastor's attention. Many of them will center around "problems" that a couple or a family seems to be having. Our theological principles of initiative and faithfulness are put to the test when these frequent occasions arise.

A visit with the persons about whom the rumor is circulating seems very much in order. Depending on the strength of the information, the pastor must decide whether to inquire directly about the health of the family. Often a visit without a stated purpose other than "to see how everybody is getting along" will yield pretty good information about the substance of the rumors. If the pastor has already established a pattern of general visitation, such calls are much simpler and less alarming. When making such visits, don't presume anything, but observe everything. Let a family tell you things you already know, but don't let on that you knew. They need to say it themselves, if something is to be said. And you may have heard it wrong from the rumor mill. Individuals should be allowed the privilege of telling their own story, rather than being told, "I already know."

Some pastors back away from an exercise of initiative such as I have recommended. They prefer to wait until people come directly asking for help. To wait is to be naive about the characteristics of human nature we have discussed earlier. Many people will never be able or willing to ask for help, but they will respond quickly when an offer or an expression of interest is proffered. We, as ministers, are among the few in our culture who have the privilege of exercising initiative instead of *having* to wait. Don't fail to use that gift on behalf of those who are struggling with their limits.

Certainly there will be times when we are wrong in our fears and suspicions. We may even look a bit foolish for expressing concern. But better to have the reputation for going *on the chance* that we can be of help than a reputation for not caring.

Counseling with Families and Marriages in Trouble

Either on their own initiative or as a result of our inquiries many persons, individually or together, will seek out counseling with their pastor. The decision of whether to proceed with their request varies with our own availability of time and sense of ability to do so. Certainly we should at least hear out the problems so that we can make an appropriate recommendation.

This book will not go into detail on the characteristics and methods of pastoral counseling, since our focus is on pastoral care. But multiple sources of supervision and other training are available. More information will be provided.

Referral

When the decision to refer is being made, the reader is referred to Chapter 9 on that topic, as well as the other chapters in Part III with suggestions about the other helping disciplines.

Show Your Interest

The most critical element in a pastoral strategy toward families and marriages is to let your interest and concern show. People experiencing difficulties in relationships are frequently embarrassed. They watch carefully and run many trial experiments to see if they will be taken seriously before saying out loud that they need help. The pastor who speaks of the importance of family and demonstrates understanding of hardships and mistakes will create a context within which people will seek help early rather than late. The earlier they reach out, or the earlier we reach out to them, the more likely that reconciliation of some sort is possible.

REFLECTION

Use this time to reflect again on your own family background and past or present occasions for helping it. Take time to become familiar with one of the family therapists mentioned in this chapter or another one of whom you have heard. Attend a marital growth session to provide yourself with a more concrete sense of what is done. All these will be helpful to you in arriving at a level of comfort with caring in these situations.

Caring for the Pastor's Family

One of the most critical factors in all this is the care that you exercise with your own family. Many ministers, caught in the conflicting loyalties of personal family and church family, do grave damage to either or both out of good motives. Watch for these signals in your own life. Remember the important developmental tasks that must be tended to. Otherwise, both personal family life and pastoral life will suffer.

For Further Reading

Achtemeier, Elizabeth. *The Committed Marriage.* Westminster Press, 1976.

Anderson, Douglas A. *New Approaches to Family Pastoral Care.* Fortress Press, 1980.

Arnold, William V. *When Your Parents Divorce.* Christian Care Book. Westminster Press, 1980.

Arnold, William V., et al. *Divorce: Prevention or Survival.* Westminster Press, 1977.

Bach, George, and Wyden, Peter. *The Intimate Enemy.* William Morrow & Co., 1969.

Bandler, Richard; Grinder, John; and Satir, Virginia. *Changing with Families.* Science and Behavior Books, 1976.

Clinebell, Howard J., Jr. *Growth Counseling for Marriage Enrichment: Pre-Marriage and the Early Years.* Fortress Press, 1975.

Clinebell, Howard J., Jr., and Charlotte H. *The Intimate Marriage.* Harper & Row, 1970.

Ferber, Andrew; Mendelsohn, Marilyn; and Napier, Augustus, eds. *The Book of Family Therapy.* Science House, 1972.

Fitzgerald, R. V. *Conjoint Marital Therapy.* Jason Aronson, 1973.

Gardner, Richard. *The Boys and Girls Book About Divorce.* Jason Aronson, 1971.

Hulme, William E. *The Pastoral Care of Families: Its Theology and Practice.* Abingdon Press, 1962.

Jones, Susan L. *Family Therapy: A Comparison of Approaches.* Robert J. Brady Co., 1980.

Kysar, Myrna and Robert. *The Asundered: Biblical Teachings on Divorce and Remarriage.* John Knox Press, 1978.

Oates, Wayne E., and Rowatt, Wade. *Before You Marry Them.* Broadman Press, 1975.

Otto, Herbert A., ed. *Marriage and Family Enrichment: New Perspectives and Programs.* Abingdon Press, 1976.

Satir, Virginia M. *Peoplemaking.* Science and Behavior Books, 1972.

Stewart, Charles W. *The Minister as Family Counselor.* Abingdon Press, 1979.

14
A Pastoral Approach to Sexuality

"Revolutions" taking place in marriage, family, divorce, singleness, and sexual roles result in many people coming to a pastor about problems that involve sexuality. One of the most important tasks of ministry is to maintain a willingness to deal with these very concrete issues. At the same time, we must continue to seek information from both theological and scientific frames of reference. They should aid us in bringing pastoral care to those who wrestle with issues of sexuality.

BIBLICAL AND THEOLOGICAL RESOURCES

Literally from the beginning the Bible deals with human beings in terms of their sexuality. The creation narratives pronounce that sexuality good. In fact, some writers point out that the creation of human persons is not pronounced good and finished until it is sexual. The differences are intentional. Further, it is intended that the two shall be related to each other as God's co-creators, cooperating in their mutual responsibility for the creation.

The Value of Differences

Perhaps the differences are ones of experience or perception, caused by the differences in anatomy. Whatever they are, they enable us to respond to each other and yet retain our sense of uniqueness. The danger is always that we will distort the *value* we place on those differences and create conflicts over status.

It is important that we be careful to deal with the *intention* provided in the Old and New Testaments with regard to sexuality. People may bring to our attention the apparent lowered status of women in the Bible, forgetting or ignoring the accounts valuing women and the occasions in which they assume leadership.

Differences bring vitality in relationship. Sexual issues provide possibility for richness or depravity, and we regularly see evidence of both. Differences are not intended to breed jealousy or envy of the other. Rather, they provide opportunity for pride in one's uniqueness and value in sharing and receiving with one who is equally valuable and unique.

A Source of Enjoyment

Not only were we created equal, adequate, and different, but we were created to enjoy the differences. When God surveyed the creation, including the characteristics of male and female, it was seen as *good.* The Hebrews, inspired by God, saw sexuality to be a good thing, to be dealt with in very specific, and often lusty, ways. The Song of Solomon in particular utilizes sexual language to portray the graphic, infatuated process of a couple longing for each other and relishing each other's sexuality.

Detailed codes were developed in the Old Testament for the enjoyment of sexuality and the protection of persons from sexual abuse. One of the evidences of sin was the necessity to cover our nakedness, once viewed as beautiful and expressive but now seen as a source for mistreatment and vulnerability. Most importantly, the enjoyment of sexuality was seen as a glorification of God. Sexual abuse of a person was and is an offense to God.

The attitude toward sexuality is consistently one of appreciation and advocacy of it as an opportunity for glorifying and experiencing the ecstasy of being loved by God. The sexual experience is one that gives us some glimpse of the depth to which God's love for us reaches. *And* it gives us the experience, when abused, of the alienation that comes from being mistreated in a relationship characterized by faithfulness.

An Opportunity for the Expression of Faithfulness

Caution throughout the Bible about idolatry reminds us that the sexual relationship is not to be overvalued. Nevertheless, it stands as one of the regular paradigms used to describe faithfulness. In the Old Testament there seems to be a view that one must be married to be whole. That view diminishes in the New Testament, but comparisons are still made between the marital relationship and the relationship of Christ and the church. The unfaithfulness of God's people is compared to the unfaithfulness of Gomer to her husband, Hosea.

So, the sexuality of our nature draws us together in an opportunity for faithfulness. At the same time, it tempts us to be unfaithful in powerful ways. Those are the concerns brought so often to the pastor.

Being Sexual and Remaining Human

Part of the human dilemma is that neat sets of rules often strip sexuality of its richness rather than protecting it. At the same time, ignoring its dangers results in debasing it and stripping it of richness and meaning.

There is no way that we can be human without acknowledging our sexuality. At the same time, it is very possible to express our sexuality in ways that are dehumanizing. Relationships between men and women or persons of the same sex, sexual intercourse, and frustration in sexual expression are only a few of the problems that people will bring to a pastor. They are seeking to be more human in the finest sense of the word, but their sexual experiences have brought them to feel less than human. Their sense of identity is at stake. It is more than "just a physical thing."

SCIENTIFIC RESOURCES

Massive research has sought to discover the causes of sexual dysfunction and appropriate treatment for it. The conclusion of many is that sexual problems are relationship problems and often have a great deal to do with self-concept. Developmental studies of identity and consciousness of self demonstrate the early beginnings of a sense of maleness and/or femaleness, accompanied by value connotations. Consequently, multiple educational programs have been launched in the interest of alerting parents, professionals, and educators to the importance of paying attention to sexual development and understanding.

Physical Approaches

While sex is not *just* a physical thing, it is physical in much of its expression. Therefore, many persons come seeking relief from perceived physical problems. These include impotence, premature ejaculation, retarded ejaculation, lack of enjoyment, and inability to experience orgasm. Even though a minority of these difficulties are the result of such diseases as alcoholism or diabetes, medical evaluation is important to rule out such causes so that treatment will be appropriate. Drug history, disease history, and psychiatric history are important.

Masters and Johnson, who are probably most widely publicized in sexual treatment, emphasize the "natural" function of sexuality in the body. It must be understood and incorporated into our sense of identity. A part of that understanding must include our physiological knowledge of ourselves, the opposite sex, and the functioning of our bodies. For instance, when we are sleeping, every ninety minutes a male has an erection and a female lubricates. Such natural functions maintain a state of "readiness" not only for sexual intercourse but for all of the biochemical activities that take place when we are attracted toward or repelled from another person. Interestingly enough, that erection or lubrication takes place with regularity in 99 percent of the population *whether or not* they have found themselves able to "perform" and/or enjoy sexual intercourse or heterosexual relationships.

Many therapies take a very behavioristic approach to dealing with sexual dysfunction. For males suffering from premature ejaculation, as an example, the behavioral method known as the semen squeeze technique helps a male to get in touch with his senses, come to understand his body more fully, and eventually learn to enjoy and control his sexual functioning. Women who experience little if any enjoyment often profit from the technique of sensate focus, learning what sorts of behavior enrich their experience and gaining confidence in telling a partner what they need to receive to enhance their experience. This technique is also valuable to males.

Therapeutic Approaches

When the concept of the self or a relationship is troubled, techniques are not always helpful. Psychotherapy often is needed to focus on a loss of interest in living that first manifests itself in a loss of interest in sexual expression. An intensified interest, on the other hand, might be a desperation maneuver to recover a sense of being important and intact. Exploration of one's history, present forms of self-expression, health, and dissatisfaction with primary relationships—all receive attention and scrutiny in a therapeutic process. A great deal of literature exists presenting varied methods on the subject.

Masters and Johnson have noted that often the primary focus of therapy must be placed on teaching the partners to learn to value giving as much as they value receiving. Another way of putting it is that the partners must learn not to be so preoccupied with self-gratification. Such observations assist us in our theological understanding of the nature of relationships.

HOMOSEXUALITY

Because of the prominence of the issue of homosexuality in recent years, it is important to give some perspective on it from the frames of reference used above. Needless to say, there is much controversy within theological circles about homosexuality. While debate continues in theological and scientific circles, pastors are called on to be responsive to and caring of persons struggling with the issues of homosexuality.

There are several courses that we can take and should take. First, we should remember that *all* of us are children of God, regardless of our sexual orientation. That is a source of commonality for us. Second, we should continue to study and seek to understand our own psychosexual dispositions, recognizing our ability to love and care for persons of our own sex as well as those of the opposite one.

Along with the first two courses comes a third, the will·

ingness to affirm our moral values about the responsible exercise of one's sexuality in friendships, romances, or marriages, remembering the high regard in which sexuality is held in our faith. Further, and a fourth concern, is the importance of examining ourselves carefully in our tendency to be prejudiced toward those of different persuasions than ourselves. It is easy to let uneasiness prod us into premature condemnation or refusal to extend a caring hand to one from whom we are different.

Fifth, we need to be willing to acknowledge any uncertainty regarding homosexuality. Or, if we are certain, we need to be willing to reexamine the issue in the light of new knowledge as it appears. Finally, we need to keep in mind the difference between moral regard and civil rights. Just as we affirm the rights of others whose behavior we question, we should be willing to stand up for the rights of the alienated and the oppressed in the sexual sphere as well. Our willingness to defend their rights does not necessitate approval of their behavior.

Pastoral care of persons with homosexual orientation is demanding whether or not there is a desire to change. They live under a great deal of pressure and need a listening ear. Sometimes they need protection as well. The family and close friends of the person of homosexual orientation are also in need of special care. Maintain a posture of being able to care for them and for those who seek to persecute them.

TWO INCIDENTS INVOLVING SEXUAL CONFLICT

A gentle tapping on my door one day called my attention to a hesitant, anxious young man asking, "Are you a preacher?" "Yes," I replied. He darted to a chair, sat down, and blurted out, "Good, I need to get married—quick!" We still had not gotten around to introductions. No doubt in response to my quizzical look, he added: "I have to get married. My girl friend is pregnant." Something in me, probably intuition, led me to ask, "How do you know?" His confident reply was, "Because her period was supposed to start this morning, and it didn't." The time then was 11:00 A.M.!

Such a beginning led to many conversations with this twenty-one-year-old young man and his girl friend. They eventually did marry, and I performed the wedding with pleasure. After shaky beginnings, they had learned a great deal more about each other, understood the facts about sex and the beauty of their sexuality. To move from "having to" to "knowing and wanting to" was a significant process for them. Now, ten years later, they continue to enjoy each other and their two delightful children in the fullest sense of the word. Our relationship began very explicitly with their learning to appreciate and understand their sexuality.

Another incident was less enjoyable. I was contacted by a woman who had just discovered that her husband had had a brief affair with a secretary at his office. The relationship was over, and the woman had left her job. Both husband and wife wanted to maintain their marriage. However, the wife found herself unable to forgive him even though she wanted to desperately. Experiencing herself as betrayed and used, in her rage she refused to accept any authentic expression of sexuality, from the simplest hug or warm word of greeting to intercourse. The husband was so overcome with guilt at what he had done that he, too, was unable to express affection toward his wife. They separated themselves from each other as completely as any two persons I have ever seen. Certainly there was anger in both, depression in both, and an experience in both of being betrayed in the hour of need. At the same time, there was deep belief in the importance of the commitments they had made to each other in marriage. The result was inability to decide to make the relationship work and inability to decide to end the relationship.

Sexuality had been a difficult issue for them from childhood. It had not been discussed much in their marriage, only "done." Now, because of its unspeakable nature before, it was still unspeakable, and they suffered for years.

A PASTORAL STRATEGY

The two incidents involved above demonstrate readily the importance of sexuality being *speakable*. Had adequate education taken place in the lives of any of those people, there would not have been the awkwardness or tragedy which each one experienced. Therefore, one of the strategic tasks of a pastor is to make the whole area of sexuality speakable between people. This involves proper *interpretation* of the nature and purpose of sexuality from our theological frames of reference. Often we will have to exercise the principle of initiative by raising the issue, because many are still uncomfortable speaking about their concerns in the area of sexuality. In preaching, teaching, and pastoral care and counseling, we must interpret and make speakable the words and feelings that accompany various sexual issues.

Second, we must know the *resources* in a community for people with specific sexual problems. Not all physicians and therapists are trained to deal with sexual dysfunction, so we must locate those who are.

Third, we must *cultivate and train ourselves* to be both understanding of sexual transgressions and willing to speak an ethical word about the intention of sexuality. This may be the most difficult balancing act we are to handle. We need to inform ourselves and submit ourselves to training so that we can take transgressions seriously but not treat them in a way that destroys the possibility for learning and growth.

Fourth, *be aware* of the intense level of feeling that is involved in sexual issues. Many people come needing to be heard. Many will not come because of their shame and/or guilt and need to be called when you hear of some sort of tragedy involving sexuality. Initiative and faithfulness combine to provide opportunities for repentance, expression of anger, prayer, forgiveness, and hope. The personal identity is a sexual identity, and the deepest emotion surrounds such experiences.

Fifth, continue to foster personal growth in insight and understanding of *your own sexuality.* Only as you come to terms with the ways in which you turn on and turn off to people because of sexual signals will you be able to use your own sexuality in ways that are faithful and full of integrity. At the same time, only through such awareness will you be less vulnerable to manipulation by other people using their sexuality in their relationship to you.

REFLECTION

Read more about sexuality. *Discuss* sexuality with other people, particularly people of the opposite sex. Seek to understand their feelings and viewpoints about sexual issues. *Examine* yourself in more depth, both in terms of your awareness of your own sexual feelings and in terms of understanding the way your body works. Make the issues of sexuality more speakable, in terms of physical characteristics, role stereotypes, relationships between people of the same sex and opposite sex, and ethical principles.

214 of Contexts for Pastoral Care

For Further Reading

Barnhouse, Ruth T., and Holmes, Urban T., III, eds. *Male and Female: Christian Approaches to Sexuality.* Seabury Press, 1976.

Butler, Robert N., and Lewis, Myrna I. *Sex After Sixty: A Guide for Men and Women for Their Later Years.* Harper & Row, 1976.

Group for the Advancement of Psychiatry. *Assessment of Sexual Function: A Guide to Interviewing.* Jason Aronson, 1974.

Human Sexuality: New Directions in American Catholic Thought. A Study Commissioned by the Catholic Theological Society of America. Paulist Press, 1977.

Jewett, Paul. *Man as Male and Female: A Study in Sexual Relationships from a Theological Point of View.* Wm. B. Eerdmans Publishing Co., 1975.

Jones, Clinton R. *Homosexuality and Counseling.* Fortress Press, 1974.

Kaplan, Helen S. *Disorders of Sexual Desire and Other New Concepts and Techniques in Sex Therapy.* Brunner/Mazel, 1979.

Kennedy, Eugene. *Sexual Counseling.* Seabury Press, 1977.

McNeill, John J. *The Church and the Homosexual.* Sheed, Andrews & McMeel, 1976.

Masters, William, and Johnson, Virginia E. *Human Sexual Inadequacy.* Little, Brown, 1970.

Nelson, James B. *Embodiment: An Approach to Sexuality and Christian Theology.* Augsburg Press, 1978.

Presbyterian Church in the United States. *The Church and Homosexuality: A Preliminary Study.* Atlanta: Office of the Stated Clerk, PCUS, 1977.

Switzer, David K., and Switzer, Shirley A. *Parents of the Homosexual.* Christian Care Book. Westminster Press, 1980.

Suggested Readings
on Special Issues
in Pastoral Care

The contexts for pastoral care discussed thus far are common and traditional ones for which ministers are called. Of course, there are many more for which ministers *should* be called. And there are others which ministers should *initiate*. Listed below are some of the special issues with suggested bibliography for *beginning* a process of reflection about them. Obviously, the references are not exhaustive. Unfortunately, some of the areas have received little substantive attention.

Minority Groups
Wimberly, Edward P. *Pastoral Care in the Black Church*. Abingdon Press, 1979.

Persons and Families with Special Handicaps
Cox-Gedmark, Jan. *Coping with Physical Disability*. Christian Care Book. Westminster Press, 1980.

Women and Men Struggling with Women's Issues
Clinebell, Charlotte H. *Counseling for Liberation*. Fortress Press, 1976
———. *Meet Me in the Middle*. Harper & Row, 1973.
Miller, Jean Baker. *Toward a New Psychology of Women*. Beacon Press, 1977.

Aging Persons

Hulme, William E. *Mid-Life Crises.* Christian Care Book. Westminster Press, 1980.

Lester, Andrew D., and Lester, Judith L. *Understanding Aging Parents.* Christian Care Book. Westminster Press, 1980.

Madden, Myron C., and Madden, Mary Ben. *For Grandparents: Wonders and Worries.* Christian Care Book. Westminster Press, 1980.

Children

Arnold, William V. *When Your Parents Divorce.* Christian Care Book. Westminster Press, 1980.

Fassler, Joan. *My Grandpa Died Today.* Human Sciences Press, 1971.

Gardner, Richard. *The Boys and Girls Book About Divorce.* Jason Aronson, 1971.

————. *Psychotherapy with Children of Divorce.* Jason Aronson, 1976.

————. *Understanding Children.* Jason Aronson, 1973.

Wagemaker, Herbert, Jr. *Parents and Discipline.* Christian Care Book. Westminster Press, 1980.

Enrichment Groups

Clinebell, Howard J., Jr. *The People Dynamic.* Harper & Row, 1972.

Miller, Sherod, et al. *Alive and Aware.* Interpersonal Communication Programs, 1975.

Oden, Thomas C. *The Intensive Group Experience: The New Pietism.* Westminster Press, 1972.

INDEX

Index